PRAISE FOR *BEYOND THE MESSY TRUTH*

"Van Jones is a light in the darkness when we need it most. *Beyond the Messy Truth* breaks with the tribalism of today's politics and offers us a way forward. In the tradition of the great bridge builders of our past, Van's love for this country and all its people shines through."

—CORY BOOKER, U.S. senator, New Jersey

"Van Jones's willingness to speak with, not to, those who may not traditionally hold his political and cultural point of view is on full display in *Beyond the Messy Truth*. In an age when hardworking families across America are feeling left behind, Van's commitment to letting other voices be heard is much needed in today's discourse."

—RICK SANTORUM,
former senator of Pennsylvania
and Republican presidential candidate

"Whether you agree or disagree with him, Van Jones's voice has become an integral part of our national political debate. He is one of the most provocative and interesting political figures in the country."

—BERNIE SANDERS, U.S. senator, Vermont

"If I say I'm actually friends with Van Jones, will that cause conservatives to read the book or just cause progressives not to? I hope they *all* read it—I disagree with Van on just about everything, but I respect him for being authentic in his convictions and for having the ability to articulate them forcefully but fairly."

— MIKE HUCKABEE,
former governor of Arkansas
and Republican presidential candidate

"We should all be listening to Van Jones, because of how deeply he's been listening to all kinds of people who are hurting in America. His vision for American politics calls forward the best of who we are, so that we can engage with humanity and solve real problems together."

— AI-JEN POO,
director, National Domestic Workers Alliance
and co-director, Caring Across Generations

"Those of us who truly believe in the power of love and aloha welcome *Beyond the Messy Truth* with open arms, in the hope that it will be read by those from all parts of the country and all points on the political spectrum. This book will help start conversations and bring people together to find common ground and work toward a better America."

— TULSI GABBARD, U.S. congresswoman, Hawaii

"What you will find in these pages is the work of one of the most thoughtful and honest progressives on the American political scene. We disagree, and our debates can get, well, messy. But every so often, we find a place of agreement and cause to celebrate. The great battle of ideas is a bedrock of our democracy—and there is no one better at this than Van Jones."

— JEFFREY LORD,
political strategist and former CNN commentator

"Speaking with heartfelt conviction and clarity of purpose, [Van] Jones proffers an achievable pathway to harmony for ideologues of both conservative and liberal persuasions."

—*Booklist*

"Part manifesto, part manual for activism, [*Beyond the Messy Truth*] is enlivened by case histories and personal anecdotes that serve as support for the author's assertions. . . . The author proposes common projects that may bring opposing sides together . . . [and] offers concrete suggestions to revive democracy, heal culture wars, and prevent a Trump victory in 2020."

—*Kirkus Reviews*

ALSO BY VAN JONES

Rebuild the Dream

The Green Collar Economy

BEYOND THE MESSY TRUTH

A MAGIC LABS BOOK
MEDIA

BALLANTINE BOOKS
NEW YORK

BEYOND THE MESSY TRUTH

HOW WE CAME APART

★

HOW WE COME TOGETHER

VAN JONES

2018 Ballantine Books Trade Paperback Edition

Published in the United States by Ballantine Books, an imprint of Random House, a division of Penguin Random House LLC, New York.

BALLANTINE and the HOUSE colophon are registered trademarks of Penguin Random House LLC.

Originally published in hardcover in the United States by Ballantine Books, an imprint of Random House, a division of Penguin Random House LLC, in 2017.

LIBRARY OF CONGRESS CATALOGING-IN-PUBLICATION DATA
Names: Jones, Van, author.
Title: Beyond the messy truth : how we came apart, how we come together / Van Jones.
Description: New York : Ballantine Books, 2018.
Identifiers: LCCN 2017036063 | ISBN 9780399180040 (paperback: alk paper) | ISBN 9780399180033 (ebook)
Subjects: LCSH: United States—Politics and government—21st century. | Right and left (Political science)—United States. | Political parties—United States—History—21st century. | Presidents—United States—Election—2016. | BISAC: POLITICAL SCIENCE / Political Process / Political Advocacy. | POLITICAL SCIENCE / Civics & Citizenship. | POLITICAL SCIENCE / Essays.
Classification: LCC JK275 .J66 2017 | DDC 320.51/30973—dc23
LC record available at https://lccn.loc.gov/2017036063

Printed in the United States of America on acid-free paper

randomhousebooks.com

2 4 6 8 9 7 5 3

Book design by Susan Turner

In loving memory of
my friend and confidante,
Priya Haji,
and my brother-in-arms,
Prince Rogers Nelson

I have fought against white domination, and I have fought against black domination.

I have cherished the ideal of a democratic and free society in which all persons live together in harmony and with equal opportunities.

It is an ideal which I hope to live for and to achieve.

But if needs be, it is an ideal for which I am prepared to die.

—NELSON MANDELA,
on trial and facing possible execution;
April 20, 1964

CONTENTS

INTRODUCTION

IN THIS PAST YEAR, I HAVE TRAVELED THE LENGTH AND BREADTH of our country—from South Central Los Angeles to West Virginia and from Flint, Michigan, to the Arizona–Mexico border. The accents may change, and the skin colors may differ. But the major problems I saw are literally the same in every part of our country: Addiction, poverty, and a broken criminal-justice system are elevating death rates in big cities and small towns alike. In a sane society, *common pain should lead to common purpose.* And common purpose should lead to common projects and solutions. This book is written in hopes that Americans of all stripes will agree that our core democratic institutions are worth preserving— and that a few life-or-death issues are worth fixing together—even as we continue to fight about everything else.

America's problems are bigger than Donald Trump. And they long pre-dated his rise. In fact, the same political parties that are failing the country today—and the same political dynasties and elites that screamed the most against Trump's ascendance— created the mess that opened the door for him in the first place.

Starting in the 1990s, the elites in both big parties pushed through policies that ruined millions of American lives—including bad trade deals, free rein for Wall Street, prison expansion, and endless wars. As a result, millions of Americans lost their jobs, their homes, and their shot at a decent raise. Many lost their liberty or their lives. And millions more lost their confidence in the future. In 2016, a critical mass hit their pain threshold—and they supported insurrections in both parties. As unnerving as it is to have an erratic narcissist in power, any analysis of his rise must start with an acknowledgment that both parties have been letting down the American people for a long time. In the industrial heartland, inner cities, and elsewhere, the status quo had grown intolerable. Something had to give.

So the messy truth is this: A rebellion was justified. But the wrong rebel won. The Trump presidency has polarized the discourse, jeopardized our standing on the world stage, and inflamed hostility along racial, gender, and religious lines. Almost a year after Trump's election, individuals at both ends of the political spectrum are growing uneasy with his tweeting, tantrums, and temperament. But many Americans are asking the same questions we started to raise on election night:

How could someone like Trump get elected to the highest office in the land?

What are we supposed to learn from all of this and how can we get our country to a better place?

What can we do now to defend decency and democracy?

And after 2016, can anything unite America?

In these pages, I offer insights and propose solutions that I hope will point a way forward. But to arrive at answers that I truly believe in, I first had to break rules that dominate the present media system. I had to blow up the conventions that say: "Always attack your opponent's views, even if she has made a good point. Defend your own side, at all costs." Or: "Expose your opponent's weaknesses; conceal your own." Conservatives, moderates, and progressives are equally guilty of this. I will admit that I have fallen into this trap sometimes myself. But this is no way to run a sandwich shop, much less a democracy of more than three hundred million people. The nightly "death match" between talking heads is in danger of reducing our national discourse to a farce.

With this book, *I choose to light a match—and torch the script.* We all know that a more honest analysis is needed. And I sense that something more is possible. We may be stuck with today's dysfunctional "politics of accusation" for the time being. But what we need now is a "politics of confession," a new dynamic in which all sides can start to own up to our own roles in creating this mess. This should go without saying, but no person or party is perfect. No candidate or cause is 100 percent pure. Neither side has all the answers.

Please understand: I am in no way excusing Trump's sins or excesses. And I am not calling for unity and bipartisanship for its own sake. In fact, I despise people who just want to avoid conflict and be "in the middle" on every issue. Elite-approved, top-down bipartisanship got us into this situation in the first place. We have had enough bipartisanship "of the elites, by the elites, and for the elites." To make any progress, I am searching for a bottom-up bipartisanship, the kind of alliances that ordinary people discover when they reach out to solve the deadly serious problems that land on their doorsteps. That kind of solidarity emerges—however conditionally—when good people help one another as neighbors, as Americans, as human beings. There is only one thing that can clean up the mess that "bipartisanship from above" has created. That is bipartisanship from below.

In my life, I have been witness to powerful work that has crossed the lines of race, class, gender, and party. I have found inspiration in some surprising mentors and in people who are bridging divides on very tough issues. I share these experiences and ideas in hopes of inspiring a more positive populism—one that puts the truth above tribalism, results over rhetoric, and people over partisanship.

That's a tall order in a moment like this. My own biases, limitations, and blind spots will be on full display throughout this book. But in many ways, my views are as unpredictable as my biography. I am African American, but my friends and family look like the United Nations. I grew up in the public schools and black churches of the rural South. But my credentials are Ivy League—including a Yale law degree and a teaching post at Princeton. I am a strong progressive, but I work closely with staunch conservatives—including Newt Gingrich—on opioid policy and criminal-justice reform. I am a clean-energy policy pioneer and environmentalist who fights to protect coal miners' pensions and healthcare benefits. I am a grassroots outsider who briefly became a White House insider. I can proudly state that I have worked for both political royalty (President Barack Obama) and entertainment royalty (the late rock star Prince). On CNN, I discuss national problems. But off the air, I help to lead a national organization that works for practical solutions. It is from this unique mix of experiences that I developed the ideas that undergird this book. I own my perspective as someone who is black, male, heterosexual, cisgendered, middle-aged, middle-class. I never try to speak *for* everyone, but I do hope my experiences and insights will be useful *to* everyone.

If you are a conservative, my liberal worldview will be fairly obvious. But I am making an honest effort to reach out and build some bridges. To fix America, progressives and conservatives need a better relationship, grounded in mutual respect and deepened by working together on tough problems. I invite you to see my ideas and proposals as the opening bid from someone seeking a partnership. Mine is not the language for any kind of final contract. I expect you to find a lot to disagree with—in terminology, tone, and even in theory. But I also hope you might spot a patch of common ground.

That's the place to begin.

BEYOND THE MESSY TRUTH

CHAPTER ONE

AMERICA BETRAYED— BY BOTH PARTIES

B EFORE WE CAN FIND THE RIGHT SOLUTIONS TO OUR PRES-
ent distress and pain, we must properly define the problem.
As painful as it might be to confront, we must acknowledge that
the dominoes that knocked over the entire political establishment
in 2016 were in place—and beginning to tip over—decades ago.
The grievances and frustrations that allowed Donald Trump to
take power have been gathering force since elites in both parties
pushed through policies that helped to wreck America's middle
class. Now we are all paying the price. In this chapter, we look
backward to better understand where we need to go and what we
need to do now.

My awakening to the discontent and divisions in America
began when I started law school at Yale University. Yale gave me
my first peek behind the curtain to see real power and privilege—
and how it operates in this country.

When I arrived on campus, I had never been out of the United
States. Before seeing the Atlantic Ocean on my trip north, the
biggest body of water I had ever seen was the Mississippi River.
Suddenly I had to navigate a universe in which my classmates

were world travelers who had been attending the world's top educational institutions since they were little kids. Many were "legacy admits"—meaning that their parents or grandparents had graduated from Yale. They felt completely at home among those Gothic buildings and other highborn children. A few students on the broader campus came from legendary families whose surnames were fixtures in American life.

I came from a small town in the rural South. The son of two public-school teachers, I had attended public schools myself—with no prior exposure to the upper crust of American society. My only claim to fame came through my maternal grandfather. When I was young, the *Ebony* magazine list of the top 100 most powerful African Americans always included my mother's father, Dr. Chester Arthur Kirkendoll. The president of Lane College in Jackson, Tennessee, from 1950 to 1970, he was also—by the time I was in junior high school—the senior bishop of the Christian Methodist Episcopal Church (CME). In my teen years, he was our small denomination's equivalent of the pope. It came as a small surprise when I realized that none of my Yale classmates had ever heard of Lane College, the CME Church, or my granddad.

The biggest shock for me was the way in which wealth and racial differences separated Yale students from urban youth who lived in the neighborhoods surrounding the campus. Being a super-nerd, I had stayed out of trouble in high school and college; to this day, I have never tried drugs or alcohol. So I was stunned to find that some students at Yale did use illegal drugs; there was even a place on campus called "mental hygiene," which seemed to function as a detox or rehab center. But when New Haven's urban youth—some of whom lived in housing projects just a short walk from the campus—did the same drugs, they didn't get to go to a rehab center. They went to prison. And when they came out, they were labeled drug felons—for life. How could young people in the same age group, breaking the same laws, in the same town, be treated so very differently? This struck me as the opposite of the ideal of "equal protection under the law," which I was reading about in the law library every night.

My disillusionment with the system was already growing.

Then came April 29, 1992.

That night, Los Angeles exploded in blood and flames in reaction to the refusal of an all-white jury to convict four white Los Angeles Police Department officers who had been videotaped savagely beating an unarmed black motorist named Rodney King. The stunning verdict sparked protests and disturbances in dozens of U.S. cities. President George H. W. Bush sent troops into L.A. to impose order. I watched the L.A. rioting on television from where I sat in San Francisco, shedding tears born of rage and sorrow. Though we were hundreds of miles north of the violence, San Francisco's mayor, Frank Jordan, declared martial law.

The jury's decision and subsequent uprisings were the defining events of my young adulthood. When I first saw the video, I felt that I could have been Rodney King. I winced at every blow that landed on his prostrate body. Had the jury convicted the officers, I would have celebrated—thinking that America was finally confronting the "unspeakable horrors of police brutality" that Dr. King denounced in his "I Have a Dream" speech. Instead, the U.S. court system seemed to be giving a green light to every police officer in America. In my mind, the verdict read: "It's open season. Do whatever you want to do to black men. Film it, for all we care!"

I wanted to do something. A week later, I got my chance.

I was spending the spring semester away from Yale, working as a law student for a Bay Area civil-rights legend, Eva Jefferson Paterson. She asked a young staff attorney and me to go to San Francisco's Mission District and act as legal monitors at a peaceful

"Justice for Rodney King" rally in Dolores Park. Our job was to stand to one side and note any incidents or irregularities, in case there was trouble. As a twenty-three-year-old law student, I was excited to go represent her.

Within forty-five minutes of arriving there, I found myself handcuffed in a police van, along with hundreds of nonviolent protesters and other bewildered legal monitors.

Everything happened so fast. At the end of the rally, the crowd of thousands had poured out of the park, marching down the street without a permit. After several blocks, the police had stopped the demonstrators and ordered everyone to leave the area along a route they had designated. Many protesters—hundreds, actually—had flagrantly disobeyed police orders and simply scattered in all directions. I was appalled.

"They are making themselves look really bad," I thought. So I resolved to professionally and peacefully follow all police instructions. After all, I was there to represent my boss's public-interest law firm—not as a protester. Perhaps I was naïve to believe that my desire to do things the "right way" would guide me away from handcuffs. But my dad had been a cop in the military; his younger brother was a police officer in Memphis. I knew there was a right way and a wrong way to deal with law enforcement.

So hundreds of marchers (and a few legal monitors, like me) obeyed the police orders. We dutifully flowed down the street that the cops had directed us to walk on. We got about one block. Then dozens of cops emerged out of nowhere, surrounded us, and arrested us all. It was a trap. They had been planning mass arrests the whole time.

With white plastic handcuffs cutting off the circulation to my hands, I ran through a disturbing checklist of everything I had seen so far. A terrible videotaped beating. An awful verdict. Riots everywhere. Cops stopping a peaceful march. Police jailing everyone who trusted them and followed their orders.

Well, that was enough for me. I came from a good Christian home. I was a student at a top law school. I had a bright future in America. But even I found it impossible to continue believing in the system at that point.

I graduated law school in 1993 as a man on a mission. You might assume that, to advance my progressive agenda, I went out and did battle with conservatives and Republicans. But you would be wrong. The truth is that I rarely fought a Republican until I was in my forties, when I worked a short stint in the Obama White House. In my twenties and thirties, my major battles were mostly against Democrats, including the likes of Bill Clinton, Willie Brown, and Jerry Brown.

People forget that Bill Clinton's Democratic Party in the 1990s was a very different breed of donkey from the one we have now. Clinton and his ilk loved Wall Street and catered to corporations. They aggressively favored expanding the prison industry. They backpedaled hard on welfare and affirmative action. Meanwhile, Republican powerhouse Newt Gingrich had a coherent governing agenda, a strong Congressional majority, and the political skill to pull both parties to the right.

In those days, if you cared about vulnerable communities, you had to swim against the strongest currents in both parties.

I decided to try. In 1996, to fight police abuse and prison expansion, I co-founded a grassroots organization in the San Francisco Bay Area called the Ella Baker Center for Human Rights. Over our first decade or so, we got a renegade cop fired. We helped to sue many problem officers, precincts, and practices. We helped reform the San Francisco Police Department. And eventually we helped to close five abusive youth prisons.

But to win, we often had to take on California's liberal establishment, including Willie Brown and Jerry Brown. I learned how to fight for people who were suffering—regardless of whether the obstacle to justice was a Republican or a Democrat.

In those days, the problem wasn't just that both parties were promoting "tough on crime" policies that turned out to be "dumb on crime." There was a two-party consensus for dumb policies across the board.

THE FOUR HORSEMEN OF THE TRUMPOCALYPSE

In the 1999 blockbuster film *The Matrix*, a man named Neo tried to free humanity from mysterious brutal overlords. His actions made him a hero. But nearly every real-life "Neo" at the dawn of the twenty-first century turned out to be ruinous for everyday people. For instance:

- Neoliberal economic policy led to trade deals like NAFTA, which helped to wipe out hundreds of thousands of good manufacturing jobs.
- Neo-draconian social policy escalated the "war on drugs," which failed to shrink drug use but mushroomed the prison population.
- Neoliberal economic policy (again) led to the deregulation of Wall Street—which resulted in the 2008 crash that wiped out trillions of dollars in value and cost millions of Americans their homes.
- Neoconservative foreign policy led to the disastrous U.S.-led invasion of Iraq in 2003.

You might call these four policies the Four Horsemen of the Trumpocalypse. The powers-that-be in Washington, D.C., had converged on a set of ideas that would have terrible consequences for the country and ultimately set the table for the Trump takeover. Taken together, they created intolerable conditions for millions of Americans, most of whom suffered silently for years. The worst part of it was that top Democrats and top Republicans embraced every one of these policies. Therefore, the stage was set for a massive backlash—inside *both* parties.

Most unfortunately for her, Hillary Clinton embraced all four of these ideas. By 2016, public opinion had flipped on every issue—from trade deals to criminal justice—so the very programs that made her husband a hero made her a goat.

Jeb Bush suffered a similar fate. His brother, George W. Bush, should have stayed out of Iraq and instead spent the Clinton-era budget surpluses on infrastructure and job training. Instead, Dubya squandered a trillion dollars on an unwinnable war—and left office with an approval rating in the toilet. When his younger brother, Jeb, ran for higher office, Americans had no appetite for putting another Bush in the White House.

I find it ironic that both the Clinton and Bush dynasties were swept off the board by a bipartisan grassroots backlash against what had once been the bipartisan establishment consensus.

There's a fifth horseman we can point to, as well, one born of *lack* of policy: The political elite in those days never created a sane approach to immigration. Bad trade deals plus no immigration reform meant that money could travel the world freely, but human beings could not. Capital could cross borders safely; people could not. Newcomers came anyway—contributing much, but risking everything.

About 75 percent of America's 12 million undocumented immigrant workers are Latino. Millions of them work every day, but they have few rights and live in fear of being deported. Meanwhile, a segment of mostly white native-born Americans seethe at their presence, fearing that they steal jobs, commit crimes, and alter American culture. In this way, the failure of the two parties to create a fair, workable immigration system placed another log on the smoldering fire of American resentment—both for liberals who wanted to see America embrace the newcomers and for the conservatives who wanted to send them back.

THE 1990S ORIGINS OF THE TRUMP CAMPAIGN

Pundits celebrate the 1990s as a "positive" decade of peace and prosperity, a triumphant high noon between the depths of the Cold War and the horrors of 9/11. Back then, they tell us, despite the rancor and even an impeachment, politicians like Bill Clinton and Newt Gingrich came together and "got things done." Those were the good old days.

This upbeat narrative persists, in part, because the "winners" always write the official histories of their times. The "losers," for the most part, do not. Those people whose wallets and worldviews were on the upswing at the dawn of the twenty-first century cherish their version of the 1990s. It puts a halo around their achievements. It justifies their ascension. And it conceals their treason.

Because this story always had another side. With one hand, America's bipartisan elites were raising a toast to celebrate the new economic order. With the other hand, knowingly or unknowingly, they were shoving tens of millions of their fellow Americans overboard, to sink or swim in the shark-infested waters of the global labor market. Many Americans sank straight to the bottom and drowned—consumed by joblessness, homelessness, and despair—with barely a peep of protest (and no effective help) from these same brilliant national leaders.

From the very beginning, though, many Americans read the handwriting on the wall and tried to fight back. In 1999, tens of thousands of (mostly) nonviolent protesters shut down the city of Seattle, to derail a meeting of the World Trade Organization, an entity designed to accelerate the agenda of global corporations. I was there, one of the peaceful ones. And let's not forget that opposition to the global corporate agenda was already so fierce in the 1990s that it impacted the presidential election in 2000. Most people remember nothing about that campaign—except for the hanging chads in Florida. But if you were paying attention, you could see signs that the backlash against the new corporate order would someday be fearsome.

On the right that year, Pat Buchanan ran for president on the Reform Party ticket. He rang the alarm over America's loss of economic and cultural sovereignty. (I despised his racial, religious, and gender chauvinism. But his fears about America's economic decline struck a chord with me and with many others.) Trump's campaign can be seen as the direct heir to Pat Buchanan's message—sixteen years later.

On the left, consumer advocate Ralph Nader hit the campaign trail as a Green Party candidate. He warned his fellow citizens against a hostile corporate takeover of American life and politics. Young people flocked to his campaign, and they filled the stadiums to overflowing. At these so-called mega-rallies, he attacked the Clinton Democrats for putting America's fate in the hands of multinational corporations. Though the actual data is unclear, many Democrats later blamed Nader's crusade for Al Gore's loss. Perhaps as a result, Bernie Sanders decided to run for president in 2016 within the Democratic Party, not as a third-party candidate. Nonetheless, Sanders's campaign can be seen as Ralph Nader's direct heir—sixteen years later.

You can also trace the Black Lives Matter protests to the 1990s' pro-incarceration policies. Bill Clinton famously declared: "The era of big government is over." But that was not true when it came to the prison system. For those caught in a cycle of drug addiction, crime, and arrest, the era of big government—in the form of expanded prisons and incarceration on a mass scale—was just beginning. Democrats and Republicans were in a footrace to see who could be "toughest" on crime, and Clinton enthusiastically embraced the call for "three strikes and you're out" legislation and other harsh measures. During the Clinton years, the U.S. prison population nearly doubled—from about one million people to two million people behind bars—with that growth drawn disproportionately from black, brown, and poor communities. At some point, young African Americans were going to start pushing back.

With these facts and context in mind, it's a wonder that more of us didn't see the inevitability of the eruptions that rocked 2016. If you import "Third World" (developing world) social conditions into any country, at some point you will get "Third World" politics. On the left, that means you will see the rise of anti-capitalist firebrands. On the right, you can bet on the emergence of authoritarian strongmen.

This is true in any country in which millions of people find themselves sitting on a white-hot stove economically. It is especially true where millions in traditionally dominant ethnic groups are asked to make room for the rise of other ethnic groups. If you simultaneously add changes in established gender roles and expressions of sexuality, then the mix gets increasingly volatile.

At some point, society becomes a pressure cooker. The economic pain will raise the temperature; cultural transformations and social dislocations will increase the pressure—until something bends or breaks. An early sign of the stress is when the political poles start to separate and pull apart. The left moves further left, and the right moves further right.

So nobody should have been surprised when socialist Bernie Sanders got 47 percent of the vote in the Democratic Party primary. And nobody should have been shocked when Donald Trump found a mass following on the right, running as a belligerent strongman.

SOUNDING THE ALARM

At this writing, more than six months have passed since Donald Trump's inauguration. Trump has in many ways been his own worst enemy—tweeting (sometimes incomprehensibly), contradicting his defenders, and inflaming concerns that his campaign may have colluded with Russia to win the election. But Democrats have not managed to capitalize on his very slow legislative start. Instead, the liberals have lost four special elections, even with all the marching and rallying and fundraising that they have generated around the country. One of those special elections was even won by the GOP a day after the Republican candidate physically assaulted a reporter asking him questions. Regardless of which side of the political aisle you are on, if you are paying even the slightest bit of attention in America today, you are likely dismayed by the tenor of our political discourse and by the dysfunction among our lawmakers. If you are liberal in America, you are probably freaking out. I wish I could say I didn't see this coming.

I GREW UP IN A different part of America from most of my counterparts in media and politics. While it's true that I have spent my adult life on the cosmopolitan coasts—over the past few decades, I've lived in New York City, the San Francisco Bay Area, Washington, D.C., and Los Angeles—I was born and raised in the rural South. I grew up on the edge of a small town, Jackson, Tennessee. When my family first moved into our home, it faced a gravel road and had a septic tank out back. In other words: no sidewalks, no streetlights, and no sewer system. I spent many Sunday mornings sitting on the hard pews of the same little church that my grandparents had attended.

My father passed away in 2008. But my mom, twin sister, and two nephews still live in Jackson. So a few times a year, I fly into either Nashville or Memphis to see my family. I pick up a rental car and drive it a couple of hours through the rolling hills and farmland of my home state. Along the way, I listen to Christian inspirational music and local talk radio. I eat my breakfasts at the Waffle House, do a little shopping at our county's Walmart, and get my dinners at Applebee's.

The middle of the country has never been "flyover" territory to me. Red-state America has always been simply "home." And on every trip back there in 2015 and 2016, it was increasingly clear to me that Donald Trump's message was landing very differently in small-town heartland America than it was on the coasts. Of course, most (but not all) of the African Americans whom I know in the South were appalled and alarmed by Trump. And even the majority of the Southern whites I know initially preferred other GOP candidates. But I noticed that most of my white Southern buddies weren't willing to write Trump off completely. He had won their attention—and even their respect.

Whenever I would leave Tennessee and return to the progressive strongholds, the disconnection was obvious. Many outspoken anti-Trump Democrats in blue states like California and New York had never actually watched an entire Trump speech. Instead, they saw only the most outrageous clips that progressive groups were posting and emailing around, in various efforts to stoke outrage and spark donations. As a result, they were filled with a furious bewilderment about Trump's appeal: "How can anyone support this guy?" That question was half rhetorical and half genuine. They honestly didn't know.

To do my job as a TV commentator, though, I had to tune into Trump's speeches from start to finish. And I realized early on that I was witnessing a master persuader at work. Yes, he made unforgivably offensive, uninformed, and bigoted comments. I hated 95 percent or more of what he said. Yet he was also often disarmingly funny and a first-rate showman. Most important, he was advancing a searing, compelling critique of the status quo—an unvarnished, unsparing frontal attack on the establishment, especially the old-school brands like the Bushes and the Clintons. And his message resonated. I could see that liberals' confidence in our "inevitable victory" over Trump was resting on a very weak foundation.

I tried to sound the alarm, turning myself into an annoyance at every social occasion—around dinner tables, at liberal conferences, at my kids' soccer matches. Once it became obvious that Trump was going to win the Republican nomination, however, I realized that my short pleas, quips, and one-liners as a television panelist were not breaking through the noise. In late May 2016, with the support of Anna Galland, the leader of the progressive powerhouse group MoveOn.org, I made my way to a makeshift recording studio, set up by young MoveOn.org staffers in a Washington, D.C., hotel room. I didn't have any big, megabucks polling operation behind me, and I hadn't convened any focus groups. I had just tried to look objectively at what was going on, based on my own experiences as a grassroots organizer and native of the heartland. In early June, MoveOn.org posted a three-and-a-half-minute version of my complete argument. The title was not exactly subtle: "Three Dumb Ideas Progressives Have About Donald Trump (That Could Make Him President)." In the end, I threw in several more ominous predictions (his day-one agenda to attack undocumented immigrants and Muslims, among them) and challenged the idea that Democrats owned the rust belt, but as a whole, the title fit the content.

The first bad idea I rebutted that day was that Trump would self-destruct through so-called gaffes. Trump was a reality-TV star. He understood all too well that outrageous statements *get you more of a following* in our social-media and reality-TV culture. "He's not breaking the rules of media. He's actually following the rules of the new media system," I said.

The second bad idea was that Trump's seeming weakness on the details of policy would be his undoing. Policy goes over the heads of too many Americans; we don't vote on policy so much as we vote for someone we believe is strong enough to fix what we think is broken. In that sense, Trump was trying out for the role of "strongman," I argued, and he was gaining traction on that basis.

Dumb idea number three? That Trump was just too unpopular with people of color to win. Wrong! This part I nearly shouted: "Only seventy percent of black folk don't like him. Democrats have to get ninety percent of the black vote to win. He can be president. Nobody is telling you that. I'm telling you that!"

Before the video posted, I admit that I felt like a modern-age Paul Revere. I deeply hoped it would become a viral sensation, galloping around cyberspace to spread my warning.

Needless to say, the video went massively *non*viral. Of the millions of MoveOn.org members, fewer than sixty thousand even bothered to watch it. It made zero difference in the conversation on the left. In fact, progressives seemed to be even more bullish on their chances than ever. The only reason that I didn't pull my hair out in frustration is that I'm already bald.

And then things got much worse: In late June 2016, the voting public in the United Kingdom chose to break with the European Union.

I spent that night ranting and raving at home about the disaster that the Brexit decision both represented and portended. My wife, Jana (who is much wiser than I am), suggested that I go on Facebook Live—a then-new feature that lets you broadcast your thoughts to the world through your cellphone. I took her advice and spoke passionately about the similarities between the Brits who voted for Brexit and the masses of people leaning toward Trump (if not already fully in his court). I ended with a plea:

Trump is real. Trump can win. Tell everybody there's a time to be calm and there's a time to be rational, and there's a time to freak the hell out. This is time to freak out! Freak the F out! Run screaming around in your underwear—up and down the street—and tell people it happened over there—and it's coming over here. This hate wave that just tore Europe apart is coming soon to a voting booth near you! And we need to have every single person we know doing every possible thing to stop it.

Perhaps surprisingly, this totally spontaneous video—shot with no camera crew, on my smartphone, while I was standing in my kitchen—*did* go viral. But as we all now know, those millions of views did not have my desired effect. Instead, most people chuckled at my alarm and panic. "Is Van Jones okay?" Samantha Bee quipped, deadpan, in her talk-show monologue.

So, no, I was not caught off guard by Donald Trump's victory. Devastated, but not surprised. My entire adult life, I had been watching the political establishment get increasingly disconnected from "the common man," "the common woman," and common sense. I had seen ordinary people getting left further and further behind. My small-town origins and my work on behalf of marginal urban populations had given me access to twin sources of outrage and disaffection—in both big blue cities and small red towns. I knew a big earthquake was coming at some point. I had just hoped it would move America in a more positive direction.

The question now is: Which way forward? Since both parties are responsible, both parties need to look within. Trump's agenda and behavior represent a challenge and opportunity for both Democrats and Republicans.

In the next two chapters, I offer some tough love to both camps—in the hope that both will rise to the occasion.

CHAPTER TWO

AN OPEN LETTER
TO LIBERALS

L ET ME TELL YOU ABOUT A GUY I'LL CALL BRYCE SHOEMAKER. Perhaps we're in Indiana, and let's say that Bryce is fifty-three years old. He is handsome in that rugged Midwestern way. Ex–high school quarterback, still in okay shape except for the damn knee. Bryce had a good job at the plant, worked himself up to line manager. The salary was decent, good enough to take the family to the Wisconsin Dells every July. Even got the kids down to Orlando that one summer. Margie loved that, loved the crowds. That's before she had to start working double shifts at the Hy-Vee. Before the plant updated their assembly line with machines and laid off Bryce's whole team. Unemployed for four years and two months—and counting—Bryce can't go to the VFW anymore. It used to be his hangout to talk with friends, to feel part of a community. He's too ashamed now. He doesn't want to talk to his buddies who have jobs, and he doesn't want to talk to the ones who don't, either. Doesn't want to go to church. People either ask about Bobby or they don't, and either way it's an embarrassment. His son, his firstborn, is hooked on painkillers—opioids—and he can't shake his addiction. Every night Bryce and Margie wonder if the next phone call will be from Bobby's wife, Maureen, saying he's gone missing again—or if this time it'll be the coroner's office.

Bryce and Margie try to help Bobby and Maureen out. In the mornings, Bryce goes and picks up the grandbaby, puts her in the Buick. He always buys American when he can. Both his uncles and his grandpa built Buicks all their lives, before the factory was shipped to God knows where. The car is not new, but it still works; he keeps it running—he can still do that. On the way to daycare, he passes the old Lay's factory, and Pillsbury, where his mom used to work. Pillsbury and his mom, both long gone. Lay's too. Kids shoot up in the back of the abandoned buildings now. Police found a body there last week. Not Bobby's. Not yet.

Macy's is closed, too. Nobody goes to the mall anymore. It's all shut down. The hunting-gear shop that a friend of his owned and the Best Buy—both closed. Chains rusted to the gates. Weeds grow up through the asphalt. He drives past Jefferson High, past the football field. He remembers when this was a good, proud town. He remembers Friday night lights.

Then his daughter comes home from Indiana University–Bloomington. Crystal's the one who made it, who got out. Who went to college and has a future. He's glad to see her. Margie makes her best casserole. They sit down together to eat, like they used to, minus Bobby. Then Bryce says something kind of dumb and Crystal jumps down his throat. "Daddy, that's racist. Don't be a bigot!" He knows he's old-fashioned, knows the world has changed, but he's a good man. Maybe he sounded gruff, maybe it wasn't "politically correct," but, hell, it's true—there are more immigrants than there used to be and they seem to be doing all right. They have jobs, at least.

Crystal's going off on him about "white privilege" and "male privilege" and "hetero privilege," whatever the hell that means. Privilege over who? Everyone in the whole damn town is white, except Lester, and they go way back. Plus, Lester's a dentist. Went to Bloomington on scholarship, and he's doing okay for himself. A lot of his other friends aren't.

Bryce doesn't feel privileged. Not in the least. He doesn't even have a damn job. No money, not much pride left. He sure the hell doesn't have any power. Well . . . almost no power.

He can still vote.

ON THE ROAD, REPORTING ON the 2016 presidential campaign, I met a dozen versions of men like this. The specifics and details vary, of course, but "Bryce's" story is more or less their communal experience, a composite picture. One of the hardest things I ever heard was a dad just like this, talking about not being able to buy a prom dress for his daughter. He had worked at the same industrial plant—hard work, long hours—for most of his adult life. No big raises, but good steady pay. Then the facility closed. Two years later he had to walk into his youngest daughter's bedroom and tell his baby girl, "I can't afford it. You can't go to prom." I think about that father all the time.

The Bryce Shoemakers of the world turned out in droves for Donald Trump because they were tired of politics as usual. They weren't the only ones, of course—many wealthy people voted for Trump, too. And a lot of working-class white men did stick with the Democrats. But a critical mass of them didn't. Those who switched from Obama to Trump in the industrial Midwest helped cost Hillary Clinton the election. After all, a combined total of only seventy-seven thousand votes in three states—Michigan, Ohio, and Pennsylvania—threw the election to Donald Trump. That is a tiny number of the 120 million votes that were cast nationwide. Many of the voters who switched were men like Bryce—who felt both economically insecure and culturally challenged in the new American reality. One of the reasons Trump appealed to men like him is that the billionaire made them feel heard and seen. On the campaign trail, he spoke their language and expressed empathy for their frustrations. Now, the Trump we see in office is promoting policies that will benefit his rich buddies more than his blue-collar backers, and a few of his previous supporters have already turned against him. But I have little doubt that come 2020, Democrats will be facing a serious challenge: Trump's bid for reelection. And at this point, to be honest with you, I'm not at all confident we are prepared to win.

Why am I so pessimistic? Because, my fellow progressives, we still aren't learning and consistently applying the right lessons from our 2016 defeat. Too many liberals are choosing to blame the election's outcome solely on the Russians . . . or on former FBI Director James Comey . . . or on bias in the hearts of the Trump voters themselves. Too few are looking within, taking responsibility for our own shortcomings and addressing the serious flaws in our party and progressive movements that contributed to our loss.

Yes, it is true that the Kremlin interfered in the election in unprecedented ways, possibly with help from Trump's team (although that last bit is unproven at this point). It is true that Comey showed terrible judgment in breaking protocol to publicly discuss his investigation of Hillary Clinton (while refusing to reveal his simultaneous probe into Donald Trump's operation). It is true that some people voted for Trump in part because they recoil at the idea of a female president; several studies also unfortunately suggest that hostility toward Muslims, immigrants, and African Americans motivated important groups of Trump voters. These are all serious issues. And they have been rightfully discussed and justifiably lamented for some time now.

But at some point—just like a would-be championship team that lost to a bitter rival—we must start asking questions about our own performance, our own mistakes. And if we are going to prevail, we must be willing to knock over some sacred cows and make serious changes in our own approach. This letter is written with that task in mind.

MY FELLOW PROGRESSIVES, I KNOW how much you have given to this country. Through your blood, sweat, and tears, you have already done a disproportionate share of the work to move America from the ugliness of our founding reality, and closer to the beauty of our founding dream.

The work has been arduous. And it has been hard on us— emotionally, spiritually, personally. It's true that liberals tend to have big, open hearts, and our hearts tend to break easily when they are exposed to human suffering. Worse still: Sometimes we ourselves experience that suffering directly. Because of how we look, who we love, or where we were born, many of us feel constantly under siege—having to defend our basic humanity or prove that we have the right to be here. It shouldn't be this way. Lesbian and gay couples never should have had to fight all the way to the Supreme Court just to be able to walk down the aisle together. African American moms and dads should not live in fear that their children might die at the hands of police officers who are sworn to protect and serve them; in an ideal world, white people would have organized the first #BlackLivesMatter rally and not left the streets until substantive changes were in place. The people who pick the vegetables, change the bedpans, run the restaurants, build the buildings, write so much of the computer code in Silicon Valley—the 11 million people in America without proper legal papers, who make our economy work—should not have to live in fear every night of deportation police knocking on the door. Women should not have to view every hotel bar and every boardroom as a minefield of unwanted advances, potential threats, and possible violence. Native Americans at Standing Rock should not have to face batons and fire hoses in the freezing cold, just to protect part of America's water supply from a leaky oil pipeline. Parents of children with disabilities should not have to fight a war with every institution their child touches, just to give their kid an equal chance to blossom and thrive.

The fact that we have to engage in these fights at all is a form of injustice in and of itself. So we get tired. We get worn down, fragile, resentful, angry. Ask us to feel empathy for any of those "left out" white workers who were so important to Trump's ascendency and many of us will roll our eyes—or cry out in exasperation and outrage!

It's frustrating, and I get it. So if today you just don't have the energy, support, fortitude, or patience to put the whole world on your shoulders—once again—I can accept that. But I do hope that tomorrow or maybe the next day you may regain enough strength to feel differently. Because we have a giant task before us. And unfortunately a great deal of the work falls, inevitably, to us.

Where to begin?

1. HONOR YOUR TRADITIONS

The progressive movement has traditionally been the standard bearer for a certain set of values, among them inclusion, empathy, and solidarity with working people. These ideals have propelled us to the forefront of practically every battle for human rights; they have been a source of our leadership in the fight for the rights and dignity of women, immigrants, the disabled, and people of color. Since the days of FDR and the New Deal, Democrats have also backed working families and the labor movement, the good people responsible for the concept of the weekend. These values have prodded us to become trailblazers in demonstrating empathy for those who have been traditionally marginalized.

But I think it is okay to admit that in recent years we have not known how to draw our circle big enough to include the Bryce

Shoemakers in our midst. Progressives do pretty well embracing the historically marginalized but not so well embracing the "newly marginalized" or the "about-to-be" marginalized. We assume that the "straight white men" don't need empathy or support, because that group has been so dominant for so long. We figure "the white guys" are doing fine. If they run into any problems, they have their labor unions, right? Beyond that, we suspect many have gotten higher up the ladder than they should have, since statistically society favors their ilk. Therefore, we aren't shedding too many tears for folks in that demographic. Besides, men like Bryce Shoemaker have not exactly been on the front lines of progressive activism in the twenty-first century. During the modern era's defining fights for gender justice, racial equality, and the full embrace of LGBT people—and even in the midst of battles to stop AIDS, end wars, or defend the environment—white guys wearing hard hats have rarely led the charge. To the contrary: Quite a few have been actively hostile. That's a painful but unavoidable fact. As a result of all of these factors, men like Bryce—and the difficulties they face—have taken up less and less room in the progressive conversation over the last decade or more.

And yet millions of men like Bryce have serious problems—major economic challenges—that once might have ranked higher on the list of visible liberal concerns. Let's be honest. As the factories closed down and the morgues filled up from overdoses and suicides, I do not recall many civil-rights groups, women's rights groups, or environmental organizations sending help to small-town America. Maybe our assistance would not have been welcomed. But I don't think it even crossed our minds. It is true that blue-collar white guys haven't been there for liberal causes. But today's progressive leaders have not been there for the blue-collar white guys, either. We have been letting each other down for a long time now.

Ironically, today's Democratic Party agenda supports working-class people as much as ever—with a robust commitment to living wages, union rights, paid family leave, and all the rest. But those paper commitments don't always translate into a feeling of personal connection between the progressive elite and voters struggling in the industrial heartland or elsewhere. A great policy agenda on a website someplace does not always convey a true sense of concern and solidarity. And a few lines in a speech can never dispel the tensions and resentments that divide America's working class along lines of race, religion, and national origin.

It is tough to acknowledge the fact that Hillary Clinton and the Democratic Party simply did not speak to middle America's anxieties the way Donald Trump did. Trump had few viable solutions to back up his words, but he did directly address the raw fears and anguish of millions who feel caught in the grinding gears of a changing world. Hillary Clinton had the substance—a lifetime of stories and experiences and proposals—but sometimes her words rang hollow. It didn't help that her top strategists believed the election would be determined by the "rising American majority"— single women, young voters, and people of color. Therefore, white guys took up little room in her speeches or vision; their faces were rarely shown in her advertisements. Clinton often had the right terminology in the teleprompter—"working families," "the middle class"—but she did not convey powerfully enough how much she held working people in her heart.

Hillary Clinton is not the only liberal Democrat who—despite being a child of the middle class—has lost touch with the sensibilities of middle America. With a few exceptions (like Joe Biden), this disconnection seems to practically define the modern Democratic Party. The irony is that many urban, coastal progressives are people who actually fled the red states and red counties where we were born. We escaped into big blue cities precisely because we wanted to get away from the traditional pecking order and rigid thinking in parts of the heartland. That may be one reason that we have not spoken as convincingly about the working-class struggles in America's forgotten towns. To the extent that those places feel abandoned, we are among the people who abandoned them.

But now we need to find the courage within to remember and reconnect. Of course, rejoining your old community in a literal sense may not be emotionally or even physically safe; people should take on only what is smart for them to do. Also, just navigating your particular workplace, family, or neighborhood may be taking up all your personal energy. You simply may not have the wherewithal to go beyond that and transform yourself into a Gandhi or MLK figure overnight. I understand. But that said: More of us need to prioritize individual healing to get past our old hurts, wounds, and violations. They are holding us back from being able to contribute fully to our country and our world. We need to develop the emotional strength and resilience to reengage intelligently and constructively with the half of America that sees things very differently than we do. It takes a lot of inner work, community support, and maybe a few Jedi mind tricks to deliberately and skillfully place ourselves in conversation with people whose ideas, assumptions, and attitudes often wound us. But our present strategy of retreating further and further into self-affirming liberal echo chambers has backfired in a big way.

Collectively, the progressive movement needs to reignite the fight for cross-racial unity among working people. As challenging as this may be at a personal level, we have a strong political legacy to draw upon. A kind of bighearted grace is one of the very best features of the liberal tradition. We need it now more than ever. Michelle Obama said, "When they go low, we go high." She was right then. And she is even more right today. We have to be wary of losing that natural, openhearted quality, of abandoning our traditional commitment to doing right by all. Otherwise, even when Trump is stumbling politically, he is still winning—spiritually.

*

We must not allow ourselves to sink to the low moral and intellectual level of the Trump age. None of us are immune to that possibility. A president has the profound power to set the emotional tone for the nation. When John F. Kennedy was president, young people wanted to join the Peace Corps because he praised it. When Ronald Reagan was president, people wanted to work on Wall Street because he valued that work. When Barack Obama was president, even the Republicans stopped going hard on their opposition to "gay marriage" and the country passed reforms to substantiate marriage equality. Now that Donald Trump is president, he has normalized a more belligerent, less tolerant tone— and that tone has begun to infect even those of us who ironically detest Trump for being belligerent and intolerant.

We must "resist" Trump—yes—and that task includes resisting the temptation to become more like him ourselves. We march down the street, chanting, "Love trumps hate!" But I don't hear much love in those chants. In our outrage against Trump, many progressives are sounding more like him every day. We must never become the thing we are fighting against. Even under these circumstances, when the president himself so often "goes low," I am still calling on progressives to "go high."

Historically, it is the job of progressives to work for unity across lines of race and class. This is not the time for us to shrink from our historic bridge-building duties. It is time to honor that tradition—and rededicate ourselves to it.

2. UPHOLD RELIGIOUS LIBERTY

As I have mentiioned, I am an African American churchgoer who was raised in the American heartland. When I moved to the cosmopolitan states of Connecticut and later California, I ran headlong into shocking levels of anti-religious bigotry among lefty activists. I literally had people laugh in my face when I told them I was a Christian. For a while I felt self-conscious about telling other activists that I preferred not to meet on Sunday mornings because I wanted to go to church.

I still hear so-called radicals stereotyping all religious people as stupid dupes—and spitting out the word "Christian" as if it were an insult or the name of a disease. Some on the left have dismissed the entire Christian faith, lumping us all together with the most intolerant fundamentalists. It's downright ironic, when liberals point fingers at Trump and his supporters for their anti-Muslim attitudes. If we are the party of inclusivity, let's start by allowing more respect and room for faith in our own ranks.

I am certainly aware of the monstrous crimes that have been committed through the ages in the name of religion or with the blessings of religious people. But secular regimes and leaders have committed their fair share of atrocities, especially during the last century. For me, and so many others, religious belief has provided the rationale for loving our neighbors, showing compassion to strangers, and living lives of service to people and the planet.

Democrats should never forget the contributions made by people of faith on the front lines during our most important battles for justice. For example, I grew up in the black churches of the rural South, listening to the stories of my elders. As children, we heard about the good, brave people who had poured their blood out upon the ground so that we could be free. We learned how police officers had clubbed and jailed them. We learned how Klansmen had shot and lynched them. And how the G-men from Washington had just stood by, watching and doodling on their notepads. In church, we learned of marches and mayhem, freedom songs and funerals. We saw images of billy-clubbed black women on their hands and knees, searching for their teeth on Mississippi sidewalks—crawling while still clutching their little American flags. We felt pity for the children who spent long nights in frigid jail cells, wearing clothing soaked by fire hoses, while their bones—broken and untended—began to mend at odd angles.

We saw pictures of black men, looking like our fathers, hanging by their necks, their faces twisted, their bodies rigid, their clothes burned off—along with their skin. And we saw photos of carefree killers sauntering home out of Alabama courtrooms—their faces white and sneering and proud.

Church was a place of reckoning and education. Sunday mornings, I listened to these stories of injustice, and I wanted to join the fight for civil rights; it was the right thing to do—the Christian thing to do. This is the fact that seems to escape today's activist crowd. The champions of the civil-rights struggle didn't come marching out of shopping centers in the South. Or libraries. Or high school gymnasiums. To face the attack dogs, to face the fire hoses, to face the police batons, these heroes and she-roes came marching boldly out of church houses. And they were singing church songs. They set an example of courage and sacrifice that will endure for the ages. And before they did it, they prayed on wooden pews in the name of a Nazarene carpenter named Jesus Christ.

In other words: The last time U.S. progressives captured the national debate and transformed politics, people of faith had a respected place at the center of the movement. Today's liberals and progressive activists forget that Christians and other people of faith were the backbone of the civil-rights movement—or they too often choose to ignore that fact.

There are exceptions to this liberal blind spot. North Carolina's Rev. William Barber of the NAACP has returned to the bottomless well of soul power that sustained the slaves and defeated Jim Crow. Barber leads the Moral Mondays movement, which has brought people of all faiths together with nonbelievers to deepen democracy throughout the South. His speech at the 2016 Democratic Party convention was one of the most memorable and moving I've ever witnessed. He said: "We need to embrace our deepest moral values . . . for revival of the heart of our democracy. . . . When we love the Jewish child and the Palestinian child, the Muslim and the Christian and the Hindu and the Buddhist and those who have no faith but they love this nation, we are reviving the heart of our democracy." I couldn't help but notice how many secular Democrats were weeping, swept up by cadences perfected in the pulpit.

The black church is not the only source of spiritual support for the progressive cause. For example, when the Sioux tribe and their allies stood strong for nearly a year in brave resistance to the Dakota Access Pipeline, tribal elders were arrested while asserting their right to pray on sacred land. "For us, it's the freedom of religion," said Rhodd, a Lakota elder who was arrested for standing his ground as a water protector. "Constitutional rights are being violated here." Activists in the camp were required by tribal leaders to respect the protest grounds as a sacred religious site and adhere to a fitting code of conduct. The unique spiritual power of these demonstrations caught the world's attention—and won the day, for a while. The Obama White House stopped the proposed pipeline, and the issue is still being fought out in the courts, under Trump. In any political conflict, soul power can be a force multiplier.

I especially appreciate Rabbi Michael Lerner's efforts over the decades to find an honest basis for progressive believers and nonbelievers to work together. For years he has been working to "build an alliance between secular, religious, and 'spiritual but not religious' progressives—in part by challenging the anti-religious biases in parts of the liberal culture." But he also wants to acknowledge "the legitimacy of anger against those parts of the religious world that have embodied authoritarian, racist, sexist, homophobic, or xenophobic practices and attitudes."

This is an approach that should be adopted more broadly. No party should attempt to rely on religious voters while disrespecting religious people. Democrats can't win without wooing more Latinos, who are overwhelmingly Catholics. We need to attract more white working-class Catholics where we can, too. We should enthusiastically welcome Hindus, Sikhs, Buddhists, and Muslims—especially as people with Asian, Middle Eastern, and African roots make up an ever-growing part of American society. And the traditional black church is a legendary cornerstone of Democratic Party support. After all, the "souls to the polls" operations—which transport parishioners from mostly black churches to early-voting sites—are often the difference between victory and defeat for Democrats. It is the height of hypocrisy for secular progressives to sneer at religious people but then run from church to mosque to synagogue on Election Day, scrambling to turn out religious votes.

The Trump era presents progressives with an opportunity to better embrace believers. As some liberal activists get more spiritual, and many spiritual people join more social-change causes, I see real hope at the crossroads. In the aftermath of 2016's crushing loss, many hardcore liberal activists are turning within and searching for deeper meaning. Some are seeking out spiritual sustenance in Eastern traditions or indigenous ceremonies. At the same time, previously apolitical "spiritual types" are getting off their yoga mats and getting involved as activists for the first time. These trends provide a growing basis within the progressive ranks for a renewed welcome of believers of all types.

We can affirm religious and spiritual impulses while opposing fundamentalism, chauvinism, and theocracy. Over time, this kind of progressive movement has the potential to win—and win big—in the United States. To be honest: It is probably the only type of progressive movement that stands a chance in a country that is still as religious as ours.

Progressives must abandon the old pattern of reducing the

Great Faiths to their worst elements, constituents, and crimes—and then dismissing all other facts and features. It is not just a stupid political strategy. At a moral level, it is a form of blindness and bigotry that is beneath all of us.

My great hope, my prayer, is that a critical mass of progressives can agree on two basic premises. Number one: Any progressive approach to "faith in politics" that ignores the awful crimes of religiously inspired people is dishonest, inauthentic, and can never liberate people. Number two: At the same time, any approach that fails to honor and embrace the positive contributions of religiously inspired people is also wrongheaded. Worse, it foolishly and needlessly shuts progressives off from our own history, achievements, and present sources of vital support.

3. RESPECT ALL AMERICANS

It is easy to point out the many ways that Trump disrespects huge sections of our country. The list of groups he has openly and unapologetically offended—from American POWs to Mexican immigrants to disabled people to women—is too long to reproduce here. But we progressives have done our share of offending, in ways that we sometimes don't even realize are insulting. Indeed, it is easy for us to point fingers at the right, confident that we have cornered the market in knowing how to show sensitivity to experiences of diverse people. But our own brand of elitism blinds us to the fact that we have become notorious for saying the most outrageous, biased, and offensive things about the very people we criticize for intolerance: conservative voters in the red states. The contempt is so thick and omnipresent that we sometimes don't even see it.

Here's an example. Liberals often lament: "How can poor white people vote for Republicans? They get tricked every time into voting against their own economic self-interest. How can we better educate them?"

The implication is that voting against one's economic interest is stupid—and that only ignorant people would do something so dumb. What is wrong with "these people"?

But do you want to know the group of white people that most consistently votes against its own "economic self-interest"? Rich white liberals! They vote to pay higher taxes to fund social programs they don't need and will likely never use. They are choosing to literally lose money out of their own pockets, without getting any financial benefit in return. In other words, they are voting against their own economic self-interest.

Notice, however, that nobody thinks that kind of choice makes wealthy progressives stupid. To the contrary: We think it makes them awesome. Rich liberals say, "My values are more important than my money. There are things that matter to me for which I am willing to sacrifice my own wealth."

And we applaud them for placing their moral values over their money.

Why, then, don't we apply the same standard when lower-income people make the same kind of choice?

For many conservative voters, the questions of taxes and social programs are not just financial issues but profoundly moral ones. They implicate deeply held values. My conservative blue-collar buddies tell me: "I don't want the government going over to some rich man's house, robbing that man, and then coming over to my house and offering me the money they just stole. That's not right. Let a man keep what he earns, and let me keep what I earn. Also, I don't want the government trying to bribe me or my family into being dependent on them or anybody. I'm trying to raise my kids right, and these government programs are out there undermining my parenting. What if my kids don't listen to me and they decide to go out there and get on drugs, or drop out of school, or have four kids they can't afford? I say: Let life teach them a good lesson. I don't want the government taking taxpayer money and bailing them out if they make dumb choices. Let them struggle; let them learn; let them take responsibility. They need to figure out the importance of working hard, saving money, being smart. For God's sake, don't be a damned fool and then go begging the government to save you."

This is not a stupid argument. I come at the issues differently, of course, as someone who supports a strong social safety net. But this more conservative view represents a considered and consistent position, worthy of respect. Lower-income conservatives are making the same kind of argument that rich liberals are making. They are willing to make monetary sacrifices to answer the call of their fundamental values. For liberals, those values are more about the common good and enlightened self-interest. For conservatives, those values are more about the importance of independence and personal responsibility. But both sides rightfully see their voting behavior as needing to reflect more than just a vulgar calculation about their immediate pocketbook needs. If one side deserves respect, then so does the other.*

Of course, respecting our opponent's argument doesn't mean we have to just accept it and give in. It doesn't mean we shouldn't argue passionately about the best approach to taxes or spending— especially in a society as complex as ours, with the stakes as high as they are. In fact, we should disagree and debate. Debate is the lifeblood of democracy, after all. Disagreement is a good thing— even heated disagreement. Only in a dictatorship does everybody

---

* I want to acknowledge that the truth is always messy. Some right-wingers are especially extreme in their opposition to social-welfare programs because they think "lazy, undeserving" nonwhites are mooching off the system. At the same time, some liberals are willing to pay higher taxes to help poor people in the abstract, but they would fight to keep lower-income people from moving in next door (as some wealthy liberals in California's Marin County are working to block affordable housing in their enclave). Issues are complicated; motives can be both mixed and multiple. My point here is that it is not fair or smart for progressives to always assume that a lower-income white person who supports the GOP agenda is doing it solely out of ignorance or malice. We need to continually remind ourselves that honest, intelligent people can disagree with us for reasons that are honorable.

have to agree. In a democracy, nobody has to agree. That's called *freedom*. It's the whole point of America. But at the base of too many of our public discussions sits the same destructive assumption: I'm *right*. And you're *wrong*. We proceed on both sides as if our side is grounded in "the Truth" and the other side is always insane and delusional. And some version of this flawed concept has become the default setting throughout American political discourse. It is one thing to say, "I disagree with you because we have different values and priorities." It's quite another to say, "I disagree with you because you are an uneducated idiot—a pawn—and a dupe." The prevalence of the latter set of arguments is why the Democratic Party stinks of elitism.

Here's another liberal favorite: "How can we argue with conservatives? They don't believe in facts anymore—only 'alternative facts.' At least, liberals believe in science. Right-wingers don't!"

I understand the source of liberal exasperation here. Even though any high school student can reproduce the greenhouse-gas effect in a laboratory beaker, the majority of U.S. conservatives reject the overwhelming scientific consensus that humans are disrupting the earth's climate. Conservative defiance on this issue jeopardizes the ability of future generations to live on this planet. It's infuriating to liberals, and it is alarming to everyone who wants to keep our only planetary home habitable by humans.

But let's be honest: All humans have a natural tendency to pick and choose information, anecdotes, and even scientific conclusions that fit with our interests and preferences. Liberals do it, too. For example, a conservative friend once asked me what I thought about "scientific studies" he had seen that purported to document "fetal pain"—or the extent to which a human fetus suffers when it is aborted. My blood pressure immediately shot through the roof. As a strong supporter of a woman's right to choose abortion, I immediately attacked those claims as junk science, cranked out for partisan purposes. But if I am going to be honest, I had not looked at a single study. As a pro-choice voter, I am strongly predisposed to dispute, dismiss, or disprove that kind of research. My automatic response is not rooted in a cool assessment of the objective facts, but an intuitive understanding of the political implications. Of course, upon doing actual research, it turns out that these claims have very little scientific backing. Nonetheless, before I knew for certain, I must admit that I had automatically adopted the same dismissive attitude that I detest in conservatives who attack scientific conclusions they find inconvenient.

I can name other issues where liberals reject the scientific consensus. For instance, I still avoid eating so-called GMOs (genetically modified organisms), even though scientists keep issuing reassurances that they do us no harm. Also, it has become fashionable among high-income parents to buy into the debunked notion that vaccines cause autism—despite study after study disproving such claims. Today, a growing number of well-to-do liberals refuse to vaccinate their kids. As a result, wealthy enclaves as well as impoverished communities are suffering outbreaks of mumps, measles, and other diseases that had almost been eradicated. Conservatives are endangering future generations with their climate denial. And liberal anti-vaxxers are jeopardizing present ones.

Liberals claim to be shocked and appalled by Republican voters' capacity to forgive Trump for seemingly anything and everything. That phenomenon drives me nuts, as well. And yet we should probably look in the mirror on this one, too. While Barack Obama never came close to the kind of shenanigans that Trump pulls off on a daily basis, Obama did do things when it came to surveillance, drone strikes, and jailing whistle-blowers that progressives would never accept from a Bush or a Trump. After all, more immigrants were deported under Obama than under any other U.S. president—more than under Clinton's and Bush's tenure combined. And while liberals were rightfully infuriated when Trump bombed Syria within his first few weeks as president, many were willing to turn a blind eye when President Obama and Secretary of State Hillary Clinton launched more than ten times the number of drone strikes as George W. Bush, resulting in the death of thousands of civilians, including children. The Iranian American poet Solmaz Sharif wrote her stunning poem "Drone," a post-2016 favorite at resistance gatherings across the country, in response to Barack Obama's drone strikes—not Trump's.

I am not arguing that any of this is right, on either side. Nor am I trying to absolve conservatives of their sins against science or the earth. My only point is that we all suffer from biases and willful blind spots. Progressives like to pretend that our side is noble, wise, and Spock-like in our devotion to reason, whereas the other side is full of crazy, irrational people. This posture makes liberalism toxic to half of the country. While we should challenge conservatives for cherry-picking studies that affirm and confirm their own policy preferences, we need to acknowledge that such behavior is a universal human problem—not a special character flaw that afflicts only one side of the partisan divide.

It is elitist to crack jokes that imply that all Republicans are insane. Or uneducated. Or bigoted. It is elitist to assume that anyone who disagrees with us is either a bigot or a dummy or both. It is elitist to refer to the red states as Dumb-fuck-istan. Expressing pity, contempt, or disdain for red-state voters has to stop being the price of admission into the club of liberalism.

If we seriously want to solve any of the mounting problems we face—or even just be better partisans—we need some spaces where we listen to one another and show up humble enough to accept the fact that we might have something to learn. We need to have conversations that proceed according to a different set of operating instructions. The unspoken imperative should be this: I *want* to understand you. And I *want* you to understand me—whether or not we ever agree.

Big disagreements are fine. It's *how* we disagree—with our big egos, our big agendas, and our big attachments to smashing the other side to bits—that is ruining American politics.

We can disagree with conservatives. And we should. But we should stop disrespecting them.

4. FIX THE PARTY

Democrats spent a lot of time laughing at Republicans in 2016.

We saw the GOP as crippled by a three-way split between moderates, negative populists, and Tea Party extremists. We joked that their primary debates—with more than a dozen candidates—looked like reality-TV competitions or game shows. Trying to find the best language to describe their troubles, we threw around terms like "clown car" and "train wreck."

Well, now it looks like we should've focused more on our own challenges. Hiding in plain sight was a very disturbing fact. Despite Barack Obama's inspirational victories in 2008 and 2012, and even during his historic presidency, the Democratic Party had been dying a quiet death. Reflecting on the aftermath of Trump's victory, the *Observer's* Michael Sainato noted:

> Since 2008, Democrats went from 58 seats in the Senate to 48 seats, 257 seats in the House to 194 seats, 29 governors to 16 governors, and 4,082 state legislative seats to 3,129. At the state level, Democrats are at their weakest point since 1920. Across the board, Democrats are at their weakest electoral position since the Civil War.

Nicole Narea and Alex Shephard wrote in *The New Republic*:

> In November [2016], the party lost control of state legislatures in Iowa, Minnesota, and Kentucky. The state senate in Connecticut, which had been firmly blue, is now evenly split. Re-

publicans ousted Democratic governors in Missouri, New Hampshire, and Vermont. All told, Democrats surrendered about 30 seats in state legislatures. They now hold majorities in just 31 of the country's 98 legislative bodies, and only 15 of the nation's governors are Democrats. The losses in November are part of a sharp and unprecedented decline for the party at the state level. Since Obama took office eight years ago, Democrats have lost over 800 seats in state legislatures. For the first time in history, they do not control a single legislative chamber in the South. Overall, the party is now at its weakest point at the state level since 1920.

Though 2016 was a calamity, it was long in the making. I have spent a great deal of time trying to find out what went wrong in 2016, in particular.

To prepare for my CNN show *The Messy Truth,* I traveled to numerous states, trying to understand why Hillary Clinton lost an election that most pollsters said she would win. On one trip, I flew to Detroit to get to the bottom of why Michigan, which had gone to Obama during both of his elections, voted for Trump (by a margin of ten thousand measley votes). I found out one reason was that two hundred thousand more whites (who make up 75 percent of the population in the state) voted for third and fourth parties, like the Libertarian Party and the Green Party. As election analyses later revealed, Trump was much better at mobilizing Michigan's lapsed (people who hadn't voted in recent elections) and new voters than Clinton was.

But another fact got my attention: Analysis showed that Hillary Clinton severely underperformed Obama in the Michigan counties with high numbers of black voters. Those counties contained 37 percent of the state's voters. I wanted to know where she went wrong with African Americans in the microcosm of Michigan, since they are a mainstay for the Democratic Party nationwide.

In Detroit, I spent time with Rev. Charles Williams, of King Solomon Baptist Church. He was a grassroots organizer on the ground for Barack Obama in 2008 and 2012. He's an important man in his community, though he's a low-profile kind of guy. He's got big shoulders, a deep, serious voice, and a sly sense of humor. The reverend is very involved in political issues that affect his parish and community.

It was a cold gray day in January 2017 when I met Williams at his church. We talked for a bit, and then he took me for a drive around Detroit. We passed the urban decay and "ruin porn" for which the city recently has become famous: empty buildings, grown-over lots, abandoned houses collapsing on themselves. But he also showed me where the people there still held themselves together in churches and community centers. As we drove, I asked him what he thought the main differences were between how the Democrats had campaigned in Detroit during Obama's two victorious runs and Hillary Clinton's losing one.

He didn't have to think about his answer. Williams told me how close his relationship had been with the person who ran Obama's campaign in Michigan in 2008. He knew the guy by name: Michael Blake. And he talked fondly about how Blake had visited him at Williams's church and welcomed Williams when he visited the campaign headquarters.

I smiled to myself. I knew Michael Blake very well. We'd served together in the Obama White House. He's now a rising star in the Democratic Party, recently elected to the New York state legislature. I wasn't surprised that Blake had left such a positive and lasting impression on Rev. Williams.

"I could also tell you who ran Michigan for Obama in 2012," Williams continued. "I could call that person right now. But to this day"—and our conversation took place months after the election—"I have no idea who was in charge of Michigan for Hillary Clinton. Never met 'em."

I was stunned to hear this. Flabbergasted, really. Most presidential campaigns would see a two-time leading volunteer like Williams as worth his weight in platinum. It would be political malpractice to fail to build the next campaign around that kind of local talent, experience, and dedication.

"I used to go to the campaign headquarters a couple times a week for Barack Obama," Williams went on. "And it was full to overflowing—"

I interrupted him. "And so was Hillary Clinton's headquarters empty?"

He looked at me blankly. "I don't know," he said.

I was floored. "What do you mean, you don't know?"

"I have no idea where Hillary Clinton's headquarters was in Detroit," Williams said. "No idea. And I've lived here forever."

I suddenly realized that a theme we had casually discussed on the air had had catastrophic impacts on the ground in Michigan. CNN reported a few times that, since polling data showed Clinton as almost certain to win Michigan, her campaign was not going to waste a lot of resources in that state.

I'd always thought it was a bad idea for the Clintons to take the rust belt, especially Michigan, for granted. Bernie Sanders beat Hillary Clinton badly there, in a come-from-behind upset in the primary. The Clintons were linked to the hated NAFTA trade deal, and that association made their brand toxic to many rust-belt voters.

But I hadn't focused on the practical consequences of that decision. I told the minister, "Well, I think the reason that maybe there wasn't as big a push here is because Hillary Clinton had a billion-dollar data operation that showed that Michigan was in the bag."

He looked at me and chuckled. "Data? Data don't vote! You actually have to get out here and talk to real people and help those people make the decision to stand in long lines in the cold. You have to convince people that it is worthy to do something that may or may not ever pay off for them. People stand in those lines because of the organization. They do it because of the individual people who reach out to them. They do it because of local 'shot callers,' not just in different neighborhoods but all the way down to the block level, who have been pulled into the campaign. And those people then move the masses. Data can't do that."

"Data don't vote." That one phrase sums up the whole 2016 election. It was the entire problem with Clinton's approach.

Since Obama's election, Democrats have increasingly fallen in love with data and analytics. The disciplined, geek-powered operation of Obama's campaign manager, David Plouffe, was given huge credit for helping Obama defeat both Clinton and John McCain in 2008. But how did a party that performed so well in 2008 and 2012 get so much wrong in 2016? With Obama, the campaign was data smart, but it had a human heart. The Clinton campaign seemed solely tactical and driven by a new breed of operatives. Big data gurus, they saw themselves as masters of the almighty algorithm. They looked down on people who got their insight from other sources—like talking to real people. I started calling these smug geniuses "the data dummies."

During the campaign, I spoke to several Democratic operatives and pleaded with them to take the Trump threat more seriously, based on what I was seeing on the campaign trail. I was not alone; those with grassroots connections were screaming, after talking to people, that support for Clinton was softer than the polls suggested. African American, Latino, and labor activists were getting desperate—practically begging for more dollars and more help in key states. But the people who held the purse strings looked askance at these requests—as if local organizers were just grifters, needlessly trying to line their own pockets with some extra campaign cash. Instead of listening to the experts on the ground, the DNC and Hillary Clinton's staff just dismissed the doubters as "bed-wetters." The response they consistently gave me: "Our data doesn't support your concerns."

In a last-ditch effort to unlock dollars for grassroots organizers, I joined with other influential African Americans in a high-stakes meeting with top Democratic Party operatives in the early fall of 2016. I warned everyone assembled: "Your predictive models for African American turnout are way off. You should not be referencing the sky-high levels of black turnout we saw in 2008 and 2012, when we had Obama on the ballot. You should be modeling 2016 after the numbers from 2004, 2010, and 2014, when Obama's name was not on the ballot—and we lost! Without a major infusion of support, black turnout will not be there this time." Latino activists were making similar pleas.

It was infuriating. They ignored warning after warning from flesh-and-blood activists, people who saw the handwriting on the wall. Politics is an art, not just a science. In 2016, the analysts got it wrong, and the intuitives got it right. There needs to be more room to have data enriched by people connected to the base.

Best advice for 2020?

1. First—as we have already discussed—dethrone the data dummies and pay more attention to the wisdom of grassroots activists.
2. Next, invest more in the African American community, to preserve the strongest pillar of the Democratic Party.
3. Third, heal the divide between the Hillary Clinton camp and the Bernie Sanders insurgents.

Immediately after the election, a great debate broke out inside the Democratic Party:

Should the party focus more on racial minorities, or should it focus more on working-class white voters? This is a stupid debate—because the people who control the party's money do not invest much in either group. Instead, they spend the money on costly consultants who give the dollars to expensive pollsters and ad makers. These elites, in turn, essentially set the cash on fire. A revitalized Democratic Party would get rid of most of these consultants—and invest massively to empower grassroots organizers and message makers within communities of color *and* working-class white communities. That would be the winning formula.

Respect Black Voters

Under no circumstances should Democrats back away from African American voters, candidates, or causes. To the contrary, the party should dramatically increase its paltry investments in the one community that has backed it unconditionally. If it fails to do so, there is a real danger that black voters, discouraged, will begin to drift away.

The African American community makes up the core vote for the Democratic Party, just as white evangelicals make up the core vote for the Republicans. In 2016, 96 percent of black women and 87 percent of black men who voted cast their ballots for Hillary. (There is a cultural narrative about black men being sexist, and surely many of us are, but never forget: About nine out of ten black male voters cast their ballot to have a female commander in chief.) Meanwhile, only 47 percent of white women were willing to make that same gesture.

The only part of the Democratic coalition that ever votes 92 percent for the Democrats? African Americans. This simple fact has profound implications for every progressive cause and constituency. It means that if you are for reproductive choice, your core vote comes from the black community—because black people elect Democrats, who defend women's health. If you're an environmentalist, your core voter is not some Prius-driving Ivy Leaguer listening to NPR on a coast or in a city. Your core vote comes from the black community, because—again—black people elect Democrats, and Democrats protect the environment. On immigration, some would argue that lower-skilled immigrants hurt the black community by competing for jobs held by lower-skilled African Americans. But black voters nonetheless stand in solidarity with immigrants. We empathize with their pain and persecution. And we elect Democrats who defend immigrant rights. Lastly, it should be noted that African Americans are the most religiously devoted part of the Democratic coalition; nonetheless, black voters will board voter buses at churches that may preach against "homosexuality" and walk into voting booths to support pro-LGBTQ Democrats, up and down the ballot. On every issue and cause, black voters are the iron backbone of the progressive movement.

But what do African Americans get in return for our loyalty? Very little. Democrats do not champion black causes with the same passion that Republicans champion issues that are dear to white evangelical voters. In fact, some Democrats seem terrified to advance any agenda that would explicitly serve the African American community. When state legislatures pass bills that might suppress black votes, mainstream women's organizations and environmental organizations should be grabbing their legal briefcases and sprinting past lawyers from the NAACP, trying to get into court to defend black access to the ballot box. After all, we are their indispensable voters, without whom their agenda has zero chance of becoming law. But the opposite happens. When we ask our allies for help, they tell us, "We don't really focus on those issues."

This is the dirty little secret of American liberalism. By some measures, African Americans face persistent discrimination within the very party that relies upon us for its existence. In his book, *Brown Is the New White*, attorney Steve Phillips points out that the Democratic Party spends more than 90 percent of its consulting funds (for advertising, polling, outreach, etc.) on white-owned firms. Phillips also laments that party insiders consistently underfund get-out-the-vote efforts that would move progressive people of color into the voting booths, while still preferring to spend money on TV ads chasing white "swing voters." As a result, we are faced with a sad irony: The Democratic Party claims to be the champion of racial inclusion, but it won't put its dollars where its votes are. We see a similar pattern with women-owned firms, Latino-owned firms, and other minority-owned businesses getting short shrift.

Even worse abuses take place at the level of hiring, when elected Democrats arrive in Washington, D.C. The New York *Daily News* writer Shaun King, who has emerged as a powerful voice for the #BlackLivesMatter movement, recently wrote a shocking piece, "Democratic Staffer Exposes the Soft Bigotry of Senate Democrats." In it, he highlighted the fact that not one U.S. senator who is a Democrat has a black chief of staff. Ironically, the only black chief of staff in the entire U.S. Senate works for Tim Scott—that esteemed body's only black Republican.

Writes King: "According to a recent study from the Joint Center for Political and Economic Studies, of the 336 senior staff positions in the U.S. Senate, 0.9 percent of them are held by African Americans. That's three people." U.S. senators have a chance to hire a lot of people; those who serve in top positions influence policy, and they make up a talent pipeline into presidential administrations.

The Democratic Party is on firm ground when it accuses Donald Trump of bigotry. But then it undermines its own position by failing to hire qualified blacks for top positions, award contracts to black firms with strong track records, or even invest money to build leadership and organization in the precincts where its most reliable voters live. Something is wrong here. How long can African Americans be expected to invest enthusiastically in a party that fails to invest fairly in us? Democrats seem to expect African Americans to stand in long lines every four years to elect a Democratic president—and then go home and shut up.

African Americans are not numerous enough to ensure a Democratic victory by ourselves, but our support is nonetheless necessary to put victory within reach. Democrats and progressives need to treat us like they need us. Progressives can reach out to working people of all colors, including white voters—and still directly address the needs and concerns of black voters.

The GOP is working hard to court black voters and to make inroads into other nonwhite communities. Democrats would be smart to secure their base by committing the kind of attention and resources that any enterprise would invest in its core customers and supporters. During Obama's legendary campaigns, the Democrats may have hit the high ceiling of black support for the Democratic Party. But Hillary Clinton's comparatively low numbers don't represent the potential floor—not at all. And it's a long way down.

Learn from Bernie's Campaign

The intra-party civil war that broke out between Hillary supporters and Bernie backers in the 2016 primaries left more wounds than lessons. Now is the time to reflect honestly—and to heal those divides.

The Bernie Sanders insurgents—justified as they were in fighting for a progressive vision—could benefit from some self-reflection. To wit: It has become gospel among his supporters that Bernie Sanders lost mainly because the DNC cheated him by refusing to remain neutral in the primaries and instead actively backed Clinton. It is certainly the case that DNC Chair Debbie Wasserman Schultz had a favorite in the race, and it wasn't Bernie. She gave every indication that she supported Hillary Clinton and felt frustrated by the Sanders contingent. That said, I think that Sanders's supporters have at times overstated the extent to which any DNC chair is able to fundamentally affect the dynamics of caucuses and primary elections that are held in thousands of precincts and districts across fifty states.

There is a much more fundamental reason that Bernie Sanders lost in the primaries: He failed to secure black votes, especially in the South. Had he been able to, Hillary Clinton would have been in deep trouble. The Democratic Party is a disproportionately African American party, and the Clintons know this. They have spent the better half of their lives building real connections with African American leaders who know how to move votes. It's unfortunate, as I noted above, that this strategy didn't translate to courting and mobilizing black voters in the rust belt after Hillary clinched the Democratic nomination. Nonetheless, the Clintons' longtime relationships with black voters paid off in the primaries.

After some early stumbles with the Black Lives Matter movement,* Bernie's team was able to make connections with some leading progressive African Americans. Those activists proved to be strong at the level of principles and protests, but they proved weak at the precinct level. And so, despite numerous well-known African American leftists embracing Sanders (from Rosario Dawson and Cornel West to Ben Jealous and Killer Mike), those endorsements had little impact on the polls in states where Hillary Clinton was able to run up a huge margin among black voters. There is a lesson here for the left wing of the Democratic

---

* August 8, 2015, marked the eve of the one-year anniversary of Ferguson resident Michael Brown's murder at the hands of a cop. Two Seattle activists in connection with Black Lives Matter took over a Bernie Sanders presidential rally at the Westlake Park stage to underscore Sanders's absence in conversations around police brutality and other social injustices against the black community. They demanded Sanders be held accountable and then called for a moment of silence for Michael Brown's slaying— Sanders then left the stage without addressing the crowd or even completing his speech on Medicaid, Medicare, and Social Security. In July, #BlackLivesMatter activists had interrupted both Sanders and Martin O'Malley when they were onstage at a Netroots Nation conference.

Party. Recruiting black celebrities, protest figures, and intellectuals is important, but it is not enough. To win, a progressive insurgent must build relationships with leaders and organizations that actually deliver votes in black and Latino communities. It is important for future rebels to keep this in mind.

Additionally, Sanders backers often called Clinton the "lesser of two evils" compared to Trump—a rhetorical strategy that poisoned the well against her and permanently turned off many younger voters. But in the general election, Clinton did not represent the "lesser of two evils"; for progressives, she represented the "better of two strategies." After all, Obama didn't do everything the left wing of the party wanted him to do. But he still aided progressive causes by acting as a firewall, behind which those causes were able to grow and gain momentum. Leftists would have had to pressure her, certainly—but a Clinton victory would have allowed progressives to stay on offense on issues like environmental protection, justice reform, reproductive choice, LGBTQ rights, and many other issues. Instead, we are in a full-scale panic under Trump, operating in defense mode nearly 100 percent of the time. Leftists might want to bear in mind that we are not picking a moral leader for our social movements when we vote for the commander in chief. In a general election, progressives should elect the politician most likely to respond to our pressure and meet our demands, once the voting is over. Clinton met that standard, and she deserved the full support of all fair-minded people, after she became the nominee. Sanders was clear about this. Many of his supporters were not.

Learn from Hillary's Campaign

Hillary Clinton's supporters also need to do some serious self-reflection. One mistake Team Clinton made was in underestimating how deep the divide between her and the Sanders voters had grown. When I talked to Clinton's backers in 2016, they were often quick to point out that the 2008 primary between Clinton and Obama was bitter but that the party quickly healed and came together to help Obama take on John McCain. They would remind me that Clinton's die-hard backers sometimes used the term PUMA (Party Unity My Ass), to underscore their point that they would never support Obama. But in the end, they wound up voting for the Illinois senator in massive numbers. So the Clinton backers' assumption in 2016 was that after the primary, Sanders voters would behave the same way. And they felt that the threat of a Trump presidency would compel party unity, no matter what.

This comforting analogy failed to take account of three facts. First of all, Clinton's fans were already established Democrats, with strong party identification. Sanders's forces were younger, more independent, and less tied to traditional parties or labels. Second, there was actually very little ideological distance between Obama and Clinton; they were basically chocolate and vanilla versions of the same worldview and policy vision. In 2008, polarizing divides at the level of principle had not been a problem. We faced a different situation in 2016. Clinton had been identified as a moderate for most of her career, while Sanders called himself a democratic socialist. Though their voting records were similar, the ideological divide between these two candidates was vast. A hard-core Sanders voter would have to cross a huge philosophical chasm to back Clinton enthusiastically; the same was true in the reverse. Third, for many voters, the election was as much about outsiders (Sanders and Trump) versus insiders (the Clintons and the Bushes) as it was about ideology or party affiliation. The Trump candidacy would repel some, but it appealed to others who were simply fed up with the status quo. The data dummies had a hard time finding evidence in their survey questions that the party was more divided than ever. But it was obvious to anyone who talked with any young voters that year.

Because they underestimated its importance, Team Clinton missed opportunities to build trust. For example, in May 2016, the Sanders camp's sense that the "fix was in for Clinton" crystallized after a very tense exchange during the delegate selection process in Nevada. Sanders voters came away claiming that the state party had cheated them, a position that should have set off alarm bells in the Clinton camp. It would have been a great moment for Clinton, Debbie Wasserman Schultz, and Sanders to issue a joint statement (or even to appear together before TV cameras). They could have reiterated that all Democrats, including both Clinton and Sanders, wanted a fair election. They could have promised to seriously and jointly investigate any allegations of wrongdoing in Nevada.

For Sanders voters, this gesture and others like it might have restored some trust and made it easier for more of them to pivot to Clinton's side during the general election. Instead, the DNC chair went in the opposite direction. She threw out any pretense of impartiality. She brushed aside the concerns of Bernie's backers about the process. She got in front of TV cameras and tried to tar the entire Sanders campaign as violent and out of control, based on the actions of a few loose nuts. Her statement may have felt justified in the moment. But the long-term costs were serious: Her one-sided actions made it harder for younger voters to feel that they had a place in the party, and it made them question if they even wanted such a place.

This reaction fit an overall pattern of Clinton hubris. Clinton's vice presidential choice, the moderate Virginia governor Tim Caine, is inarguably a good man. But he is not someone who could appeal to younger voters or fire up the progressive wing of the party. Team Clinton thought they had the race in the bag, so they selected someone with whom she would feel comfortable working—not someone who could help her win. It was an arrogant move, based on the false assumption that the youth and the left had nowhere else to go.

Until both sides do some soul-searching, Democrats are vulnerable to further chaos, controversies, and cleavages. Right now the strongest force holding progressives together is opposition to Donald Trump. That won't be enough. There is some reason for hope, though. Hillary Clinton's team won the primary, but Sanders's forces won the policy debate. Judging by the party platform, many of Sanders's left-wing populist ideas are now the official stance of the Democratic Party. Today few Democrats are willing to defend the old neoliberal orthodoxy on free trade or deregulation. The bold 2016 Democratic Party agenda offers a principled basis for party unity going forward—if both sides will just take a moment to notice that we already agree on a great deal, at least on paper.

5. SOLVE REAL PROBLEMS

But there is a good chance that we will all just keep bashing each other anyway. A good chunk of liberals and progressives are addicted to the bickering and infighting, rather than to solving real problems.

Perhaps the biggest immediate threat to progressives is not Trump at all but the way progressives treat one another. We blame the orange bully without. But there is a whole lot of bullying within our own ranks, too. A dysfunctional pattern has emerged in which progressives are launching mad-dog attacks against one another, especially through online diatribes. This dynamic in fact may prevent the type of coalition necessary to defend and extend democracy. We can see this game being played on Facebook feeds and Twitter accounts daily.

It is bad enough that we can't always figure out ways to work with men like Bryce Shoemaker. But many of us can't even work with most other progressives. Worse, we use public ridicule to take people to task in a way that in many cases shames, divides, and silences some of our closest allies. We are in danger of becoming the bullies who may have tormented us in our youth. We have to address and correct this "call-out culture" if we are going to build a coalition strong enough to replace Trumpism, build a viable movement, and govern. We must have a ceasefire in the "who's the wokest of them all" war. We cannot win against the worst of the right if all of our best weapons are pointed at one another.

Right now, too many of us seem to approach liberal causes and conversations mainly by looking for ways to show other progressives where they are wrong. Too many of us can deconstruct everything but can't reconstruct anything and make it work. Too many of us know how to run a protest against the adults on our campuses but don't know how to run a program for children in our neighborhoods. Too many of us are great at opposition but awful at proposition. Too many of us know just enough critical theory to critique everything but don't have the practical skills to make anything function at the level of our high standards. Too many of us know how to march against an elected official but not how to elect one. Too many of us know how to call people out but don't know how to lift people up. And this reality creates internal dangers as real as anything we face externally.

Speaking truth to power and confronting injustices are good impulses, but when people start to use confrontational tactics in their own coalitions, their own organizations, then you have a movement that is too injured internally to play a healing role externally.

Examples of this abound on social media. On March 10, 2017, when a British Channel 4 interviewer asked Nigerian novelist Chimamanda Ngozi Adichie to comment on whether a trans woman was "any less of a real woman," Adichie's response, that "trans women are trans women" and that "I don't think it's a good thing to talk about women's issues being exactly the same as the issues of trans women," elicited a firestorm of criticism and condemnation on social media. Adichie was accused of being a trans-misogynist and was chastised for speaking on issues she had no business addressing, since she is not a trans woman. One big problem here is the way in which a single statement in an interview transformed Adichie overnight from ally to enemy. The debate consumed the energy of the progressive community for over a week and earned international media coverage.

I don't mean to discourage critical thinking or dissent. Certainly, those of us who do not share the trans experience have much to learn from that community, and Adichie (and myself) may need correcting in this regard. However, the harsh condemnation following her comments did not speak to Adichie's LGBTQ advocacy work, not by a long shot. In 2014, Adichie, along with other Nigerian writers, risked her life by taking a public stand in Nigeria against the law that criminalized gay and lesbian love, making it punishable by death. She has taken a strong public stand for trans rights and has defined issues facing trans women as feminist issues. She is under constant fire in Nigeria and the States for her tremendous feminist advocacy. To call her a "misogynist" of any kind seems shortsighted.

Indeed, many international observers of our progressive infighting have made this exact point. Activists from nations where certain individual liberties cannot be so taken for granted can see the futility of our current trajectory. The South African website *Africa Is a Country* (www.africasacountry.com) and the Jamaican Man Booker Prize–winning writer Marlon James have both noted the self-defeating nature of our progressive "call-out culture." In May of 2017, James observed in a Facebook post that "Conservatives may be a lot of things, but it would be a cold day in hell before 'kill friends first, kill enemies later,' becomes their code of conduct. Progressives love to think they are at war with conservatives, but right-wingers laugh at such nonsense, because they already know you don't need to bring a gun to your enemy's suicide. I would love to place all the blame on Facebook, but that would be kidding oneself. And maybe I'm just a foreigner looking in, with a radically different idea of what arguments should sound like. But I look at you all, and all I see is a two-term Orange President."

We've all been in situations where people have been shorter with each other, sharper with each other, meaner to each other, than we should have been. The results have been less unity, weaker organizations, more brittle ties, collapsed coalitions. If you ask people what their actual experience of being on the left is, lots of them say, "Oh, we're saving the world, speaking truth to power, dismantling the master's house, seeking justice for all." But when I say, "No, no, no, what's your experience—like, on Thursday?" They say, "Oh, it was horrible." That has to change. As we focus on solving real problems, we will learn to call our allies up, not out.

The hard left has a critical role to play. They work to hold elected progressives accountable to our highest ideals. They make a point to give voice to the needs of our most vulnerable community members. Without people putting their bodies and voices on the line, especially young people, the Democratic Party might never have addressed the inhumanity of our prison system, the plight of the Dreamers, violent attacks on the trans community, or police killings of black children, women, and men. But all criticism should be aimed at strengthening our solidarity, not shattering it. I do want to encourage principled dissent and fair criticism and constructive disagreement—which is always tougher on the problem than the person. Our discussions and debate must be aimed at improving our ability to work together to solve the most pressing human problems of our time: poverty, addiction, an obsolete workforce, environmental crisis, and threats to democracy.

SOMETIMES IT FEELS AS THOUGH liberals have gone through a process of divorce from our own country—and we need to reconcile, when and where we can. I grew up in middle America. I got my feelings badly hurt growing up as a nerd in a small town. I was too emotional, artistic, and sensitive to fit in, and I left as soon as I could. Like a lot of people who now live in liberal strongholds, I fled to the cosmopolitan coasts, where I felt like I could belong. I joined some of the subcultures on the coasts that felt more welcoming to me. And I was able to find my place and find my voice in doing that.

But at some point along the way, despite my best intentions, my capacity for connection with my hometown friends began to atrophy. It showed up around the Thanksgiving table back at home in Tennessee. I suddenly discovered that I could not talk with or be heard by people with whom I had grown up. I went back to neighborhoods and churches where I had grown up, and when I got going on my high horse, the room would often freeze. People would squirm uncomfortably, and when I finished my philosophical rant five to ten minutes later, some relative would gently say, "Well now, that was a mouthful. Boy, can you pass the ketchup?" And the conversation would move on, a bit awkwardly at first.

I often say that most progressives don't have to ask the question: "How do we learn to talk to America?" We have to ask the questions: "When did we make the choice to *forget* how to talk to America? Why did we make that choice? And how can we heal enough so that those old traumas no longer rule us?"

At some point we have to accept responsibility for this country and everything in it. The country is waiting for a pro-democracy movement that can inspire it and not just critique it.

Whatever #resistance movement is emerging should be organizing not just to protest but to govern, as well. We have a broken country, a hurt country, a country that needs solutions—not just critiques and complaints. Our country needs strong people who are willing to take responsibility and honestly try to fix things. Such a movement will be welcomed, beloved, accepted, celebrated, and lauded at Thanksgiving tables in blue states and red states.

Let's build one.

CHAPTER THREE

AN OPEN LETTER TO CONSERVATIVES

D O YOU RECOGNIZE THIS AMERICAN FAMILY? (THEY ARE AN invention, but what we can learn from them is real.) With two working parents and two teenagers, the Youngs live in Springfield, New Jersey. Dad is a database administrator for the county hospital, a place where he's worked for nearly twenty years. Mom used to stay at home full-time, but now that the kids are older, she's started a part-time job at the library. Every month, they put money in savings for their retirement and for their kids' college.

The son, let's call him Keith, is still a gangly tween, but he is one speedy kid. He has the potential to be a great running back if he bulks up a little over time. The daughter, Sarah, has been into ballet since she was five but recently grinned through a chipped tooth—courtesy of her new love for lacrosse—for her sophomore-class photo. Both kids are on track for inclusion in the National Honor Society.

The Youngs believe in God, pray together every day, and attend religious services weekly. When they hear about tragedies domestic or abroad, they attend prayer vigils. Before dinner to-

gether every evening, they thank the Lord who nourishes and protects them.

Keith and Sarah even pray before their lunches at school,
which has unfortunately led to daily ridicule from a small group of
other students. Mr. Young has called the school countless times to
report this harassment, but the vice principal—who also happens
to be quite devout—hasn't done much more than lecture the of-
fenders about letting Keith and Sarah do their own thing; defending Keith's and Sarah's rights to practice their religion at school
seems to make the vice principal uneasy. It would have been easier
for him to intervene, he said, if the bullying had been overt and
physical.

Sarah got up the courage to ask the bullies to join Keith and
her in their prayers, but that didn't go over so well. Not only did
the bullying continue (and even go up a notch), but when the vice
principal learned of her strategy, he lectured *her* about keeping
church and state separate. Still, the Youngs are committed to compassion and peacemaking. They believe that violence goes against
God's will.

Mr. and Mrs. Young try to regularly attend town-hall meetings,
and they proudly exercise their voting rights—even in seemingly
inconsequential local races. The Youngs like their neighborhood
and see it as their American duty to be involved in their community. They donate goods to their local food pantry, and they also
stepped up to bring meals and extra clothing when a family one
block over lost almost everything in a freak house fire.

Families like the Youngs live in big cities and small towns all
across our nation. They check off all the boxes of what it means to
be a model conservative family: devoted to their faith and family,
committed to community service and civic participation, and willing to work hard to contribute in the classroom, at work, on the
sports field, or in the home. They defend their constitutional rights
in the face of persecution, and they feel grateful to live in a coun-

try that honors and protects their freedoms. They are financially and socially responsible, saving money to cover their costs and extending help to others in need. In short, the Youngs are the ideal American family.

But what if their family name was Yousseff instead of Young? What if the son were named Kamal, instead of Keith? Sadia, instead of Sarah? What if the parents were named Idris and Anam? What if they were Muslim? Because in my story, they are.

Families like the Yousseffs are the best citizens—the best conservatives—America has to offer. On the whole, American Muslims exemplify conservative values. Faith, family, work ethic, educational attainment, entrepreneurship, and raising awesome children (girls as much as boys) are all values that conservatives hold dear. The unfortunate truth, however, is that many conservatives champion the Youngs but not the Yousseffs. They have demonstrated an indifference to the social and legal persecution of Muslim Americans, and in some cases they have openly supported policies and rhetoric that threaten the rights and livelihoods of families like the Yousseffs.

The November 2016 election results confirmed the worst fears that many Muslims have about this country. During the campaign, the Republican candidate made his attitude toward Muslim immigrants and refugees clear: He wanted to ban them from setting foot on U.S. soil. He also promised to establish a registry of all Muslims currently living within U.S. borders, including hardworking citizens like the Yousseffs. He frequently drew on Islamophobic rhetoric to stir up fear and anxiety among voters, turning kids like Kamal and Sadia into potential terrorists in the minds of his supporters. Despite these and other threats to Muslim Americans, millions of conservatives cast a vote for Donald Trump. Whether they truly fear Muslims or merely value other things more than protecting their rights, this vote expresses a deep threat to many of the values that conservatives hold most dear. On election night, one of my Muslim friends texted me: "Should I just leave the country now, before things get worse?" Honestly, in that moment, I didn't know what to tell her. I'm still not sure.

Indeed, within a week of taking office, President Trump issued a travel ban that suspended admission of nearly all refugees and restricted visas for nationals of Libya, Somalia, Sudan, Syria, Iran, Iraq, and Yemen. Anam Youseff's mother could be in Yemen, and she could be sick. The family would be devastated that the United States—their home—would restrict her travel or theirs to visit her.

All conservatives should be outraged by this attempted constitutional breach, and yet I've seen only a handful speak up.

Of course, the United States faces grave challenges from Islamist extremists and indeed from violent extremists of all stripes. I do not mean to downplay these threats. Yet ISIS grows stronger every time the United States seems as hostile to all Muslims. The United States should oppose distortions of Islam that call for murder, rape, sexual violence, and terrorism. But our greatest asset is a strong protection of religious liberty and an undying commitment to those citizens who comply with our laws and contribute to our communities. Indeed, our country was founded by devout believers ousted from their communities because of their religious practices. America was established as a safe haven for free religious exercise, and when we fail to defend our Muslim brothers and sisters we threaten the very foundation of our nation.

By proudly recognizing and defending the successes of families like the Youseffs, we combat the ISIS propaganda that "America hates Islam." Stories like theirs not only rebut these lies, but they also offer proof that America's model—a free, open, and multi-faith democracy—works better for Muslims than anything jihadists have to offer.

Unfortunately, I do not see conservative pundits and politicians emphasizing these stories. In many cases, I see conservatives doing the opposite, fanning anti-Muslim hysteria. In other cases, I hear nothing at all—the silence of indifference. Except for a few brave Mormon voices, I rarely hear conservative voices defending—and proudly identifying with—Muslim American families whose values align so closely with their own. Why is this the case?

This is an honest question. Families like the Yousseffs embody the American dream and model the virtues of the conservative American family. Why, then, do conservatives support a president who openly threatens their fundamental rights?

DEAR CONSERVATIVES, I'M NOT here to scold anyone but instead to spark a meaningful conversation. As I've said countless times, I believe that this country needs both liberals *and* conservatives. And we need both traditions at their best and highest expressions, especially now. We might have different ideas for how to approach a crisis, but of this I am sure: We need the best ideas from all sides to get to the best solution. Our constitution is a product of passionate disagreement among strong advocates for different positions and constituencies. Innovation does not come from insular agreement but from individuals with different ideas coming together to solve problems using all the tools and ideas at their disposal. As we tackle our country's most pressing problems, we need intelligent, dedicated people on both sides.

Of course, conservatism in America is as multifaceted as the millions of individuals who make it up. In a two-party system, Democrats and Republicans both struggle to find coherence and unity within our big tents. But conservatives in America share some important common values: a belief in a smaller role for centralized government and a larger role for local or individualized choice, an emphasis on religious liberty and protection for constitutional rights, a commitment to the nuclear family as a critical institution for encouraging the stability of our society and the growth of our young citizens, a concern with fiscal responsibility and prudent budgeting, and a deep pride in our nation's great political institutions and cultural traditions.

These values are fundamental to America's past, present, and future. Liberals may not want to admit it, but we need the challenge and counterbalance of the conservative viewpoint. Conservatives view the role of government differently and prefer a different set of tools to solve problems. But the tension can be useful. For example, liberals want to root out injustice and discrimination against historically marginalized people, so we come up with legislation. Then conservatives warn us about the downsides and the dangers—the unanticipated consequences, the unexpected costs, and the bureaucratic inefficiencies that may make a mockery of any new social program. The resulting debate can lead to a better program—or no program at all, if the original proposal was ill-conceived. Liberals want a federal government strong enough to protect our nation's most vulnerable citizens, but sometimes we need reminders of the power and sometimes the primacy of local initiatives. Conservatives generally do a better job than do liberals of upholding the importance of community, churches, and families. Yes, even as liberals try to open doors to different ideas of what a family can look like, conservatives are most passionate in explaining why family matters so much in the first place. Liberals need conservatives to remind us that there may still be important differences between the way boys and girls learn, even while we work to make sure that gender no longer limits what any young person can accomplish. Conservatives ask important questions like, "How much does this cost? Who is going to pay for it? And why should the government be doing this in the first place?" Frustrating though these queries may be for liberals, principled conservative opposition can force progressives to improve programs or even to seek solutions outside the federal government—within states, towns, churches, businesses, neighborhoods, and even families. The fact that conservatives fight to withhold federal dollars can sometimes force creative solutions that—over the long term—expand the menu of options for effective change. When advanced from a place of high principles, the challenge from conservatives actually helps keep the progressive cause more lean, honest, and innovative.

It may be hard to admit, but conservatives need liberals just as much. Conservatives want policies that bolster economic liberty and free-market enterprise, but America cannot be great if we do only things on which corporations can make a nice profit. You need liberals to point out key differences between private goods and the public good—and to raise questions about whether private companies are always in the best position to meet the needs of all citizens, especially the poorest and most vulnerable, who cannot pay. Conservatives want to limit the size of government, but you need liberals to remind you that clean air, clean water, safe products, inspected food, nonlethal workplaces, and smog-free cities are all products of government protection—which your constituents like quite a bit.

My point is: We need each other. I will keep working to beat you on Election Day. But I don't want you to stop being conservative. I'm not trying to convince you to come around to "my side" of things. What America needs in the age of Trump is not fewer of you but instead more and better conservatives with the conviction to stay true to your core values.

Where to begin? Let's stick with the same areas of work that I have suggested to my fellow liberals: by honoring your traditions, upholding religious liberty, respecting all Americans, fixing your party, and, finally, by turning your attention to solving real problems.

1. HONOR YOUR TRADITIONS

Conservatives have traditionally shown deep respect for our country's political institutions. You value and respect the vision laid out by our founders, particularly their belief that strong checks and balances should stand in the way of drastic and possibly ill-considered reform. You have typically emphasized incremental change, fiscal responsibility, and restraint in how legislation ought to be designed, incorporating the capacities and ideas of nonprofit, for-profit, and locally based entities alongside government initiatives. More than anything, you place great value on protecting and upholding the foundational liberties enshrined in the Constitution, particularly the rights to free speech, movement, association, and religion.

Our political institutions and individual freedoms are under siege. Yet this danger does not come primarily from college-aged social-justice warriors on the left but rather from blind partisan loyalty on the right. The Trump administration has disrespected our most cherished institutions, including the independent court system and the free press. It has bucked centuries-old expectations of ethical transparency. It has torn down the solid walls between legitimate governance on behalf of the people and the corrupt use of power to bolster one's private enterprise. My conservative friends: The Trump administration is discarding your traditions and heritage. When you will come to your own defense? My plea is not that you join the liberal cause but that someone please find the courage to champion the conservative cause once again.

Traditionally, conservatives have emphasized limiting the power of the central government. You value and respect our founders' vision of divided branches of government. You value incremental change, considering the slow pace of new legislation and the multiple checks and balances to be a necessary feature of the system, not a bug in the software of American democracy. These commitments stem from a deep reverence for the vision of the founders. Acting from a place of uncertainty and attempting to construct a model for government never before seen, these men came to a series of extraordinary compromises and agreements that form the basis for our government. Their primary aim? To create a system that limits tyranny in all its forms. With the tyranny of the English king fresh on their minds, they wanted to make sure that no person or group had arbitrary power over American citizens. They limited executive power and enshrined in the Constitution key rights—including speech, association, and religious practice.

You have to ask yourself, then: What would our founders say if they traveled through time and landed in 2017? Would they approve of a U.S. president attacking the credibility of independent judges merely on the basis of their heritage, as candidate Trump questioned the impartiality of Gonzalo Curiel in 2016? Would they stand by idly as the executive branch tramples on the rights of the press, limiting reporters' access to the White House? Some of these issues and challenges pre-date Trump; many will surely outlast his tenure. The nation needs consistent, conservative counsel on all of them.

It is essential that conservatives join the fight to protect free speech and free expression from its greatest threat: a president who demeans journalists, bans media outlets from press briefings, threatens to cancel press briefings altogether, and dismisses media reports that run counter to his narrative as "fake news." These attacks make it difficult for citizens to empower themselves with knowledge and make independent decisions. They erode the power of our nation's most essential check on government, the independent press. And they endanger one of our most essential constitutional rights—the right to free expression.

To be clear, I believe that like any other citizen, a president should be able to direct criticism at reports he feels are incorrect or unfairly portrayed. Some of my own statements have been unfairly inflated by a media outlet or two, and it is also my right to complain. But the minute someone with Donald Trump's power and pulpit categorically denounces all critical media coverage as fake, he is creating a false alternative reality for half the nation and ensuring that our nation remains divided.

Now, I must say that the idea of "free speech" has become a muddled concept lately. Both liberals and conservatives rely on free speech when we want to make claims that are offensive to our opponents. But we tend to set aside our convictions when we ourselves are offended. Take the recent example in New York City of the Public Theater's production of *Julius Caesar,* where the director made the artistic decision to depict Julius Caesar using traits associated with Donald Trump. A similar, Obama-themed version of the play had been put on elsewhere, years earlier, without incident. But within hours of the announcement of a Trump-themed production, conservatives wanted to ban it. Constituents put pressure on supporters to strip the company of its funding. Delta Air Lines, one of the Public Theater's major supporters for decades, withdrew its support under pressure from customers.

Yet these same conservatives get passionate when they defend free speech on college campuses. Recently, liberal students have been shouting down conservative speakers or successfully pressuring them to cancel their appearances. Conservatives have been screaming bloody murder about these incidents. Let me say that I understand student outrage at seeing their university give a platform to views they find dangerously racist, sexist, homophobic, or anti-Jewish. That said, I have been outspoken in my view that shutting down offensive speech—either through disruptive protest or by university fiat—is almost always wrongheaded. A well-rounded citizen must develop the poise and skill to speak her or his own truth and win tough arguments, even in the face of outrageous provocation. It is better to counter offensive speech with illuminating speech than to make martyrs out of fools by censoring them. Theaters and college campuses should challenge minds and spark thoughtful, impassioned conversation.

Of course, there are lines that nobody should cross. Expression that directly threatens or intimidates—say, by drawing a swastika on a classmate's dorm-room door or hanging up a noose—should always be punished. No administrator or teacher should make blatantly racist or sexist remarks that make students of color and/or female students feel like second-class citizens in their own classrooms. There is a difference between sharing controversial ideas and issuing targeted threats or undermining students. But the theater has served as society's classroom for millennia, offering representations of the derogatory and the divine to get citizens thinking about issues of right and wrong. And a college is doing its job if its students are routinely offended, forced to confront ideas and beliefs that are salacious, inflammatory, or unfamiliar. Those confrontations will compel audience members to develop the ability to articulate why they are offended and then develop the capacity to argue back. That's the whole point of a modern education. We want students to be physically safe, but emotionally and intellectually strong. I would no sooner ban offensive speech from a campus than I would ban weights from a gym. It is by meeting tough mental and physical challenges that we grow. On this, I am sure we agree.

That said, though, I think we spend way too much time on these campus skirmishes. When college students protest speakers they disagree with, conservative pundits denounce them as the "snowflake generation," too emotionally vulnerable to handle a challenging point of view. It's as if conservatives actually believe that student protesters represent a greater threat to free speech than government encroachment. The real danger we're now facing is the "snowflake president" we have in Donald Trump, a man who lashes out at perceived slights and whose threats on the free press get more authoritarian with each passing day.

Our constitution was created to limit tyrants and would-be dictators. Nobody was worried about whiny students. Freedom of speech was protected in the Bill of Rights because our founders knew then what we see now in countries like Russia and Iran—that without extreme vigilance, rulers with political power will use that power to silence ideas that get in their way. This pattern is the norm, and America's history of free speech is the exception. Conservatives claim to hate tyranny and love liberty. Here is the chance to prove it; nothing will better teach students about the importance of defending unpopular speech from abusive authorities than conservatives bucking their own party to protect American traditions.

Furthermore, we need conservatives to defend our democratic republic itself. I grew up in the 1980s. As you can imagine, I was no huge fan of President Ronald Reagan; like most liberals, I found his anti-communist rhetoric about Russia to be over the top and bombastic. We were afraid he was going to start a nuclear war. But nobody doubted Reagan's patriotism or his commitment to democracy. He wanted the United States to remain strong and independent. He refused to allow Russia or any other foreign power to weaken our system of government. I believe that if he were alive today, Reagan would be incensed by the proven Russian attempts to interfere in the 2016 U.S. elections. While we can debate whether Russian meddling influenced the outcome of the election, and to what extent, if any, Trump administration members colluded with this meddling, it is transparent that Russian officials intentionally sought to influence America's free and fair election process. This attack on our most sacred institution, voting, should be unacceptable to anyone—liberal or conservative.

Reagan would be horrified to learn that members of his party joked that one of his peers and his party's presidential nominee were under Russian influence. Yet Republican Majority Leader Kevin McCarthy did that (in June 2016, a month before Trump clinched the Republican nomination). Reagan would have advocated openly for an independent investigation into Russian electoral interference. Conservatives have always placed a priority on defending America from our nation's enemies and protecting our democracy from foreign powers, making this commitment a centerpiece of political campaigns. More Republicans are now calling for an independent investigation. As sources reported Trump's interest in firing Robert Mueller, the special counsel in charge of that investigation, Republican leaders began to defend Mueller, insisting that he stay on in the role. Senator Lindsey Graham said that firing Mueller would be a "disaster," and Senator Susan Collins noted that it would "certainly be an extraordinarily unwise move." I applaud their firmness on this issue and hope they serve as models for Republicans across the country.

We know that the current government of Russia openly tampers with elections, controls the press, lies to its people, and represses basic freedoms like speech, movement, and religious belief. If Russia did indeed work with individuals in our president's administration to attempt to secure his election, this threatens American freedom and democracy.

Finally, I urge you to continue to defend your tradition of prizing ethical leadership. Liberals and conservatives both strongly believe that America's government must be "of the people, by the people, for the people." Yet with the blurred or nonexistent boundaries between the Trump administration and the for-profit Trump enterprises, I have to ask: Whose interests are truly being served?

To demonstrate that their own financial interests will not influence political decisions, all modern presidents have placed their assets in a blind trust for the duration of their terms; they did this to remove all doubt that they were acting in anything but what they perceived as the best interests of the republic. Trump, on the other hand, has refused to honor this tradition. Instead, he set a troubling new precedent: He turned the job of running his businesses over to his two sons, Eric and Donald Trump, Jr., giving only verbal assurances that he wouldn't discuss their family business with them and would instead step far back and let them run his show. Even if he makes good on that promise and never discusses Trump business with his sons while serving as president, he actually still has access to the organization in another way: On February 10, 2017, a little less than a month after Donald Trump was sworn into office, the Trump Organization made quiet changes to their corporate documents to allow "the Trustees [to] distribute net income or principal to Donald J. Trump at his request." In essence, this revised language allows for Trump to draw funds from any of his four hundred businesses without sharing his reasoning with a soul or disclosing any transfer of funds to the voting public.

The list of questionable ethics issues goes on: Trump's business projects in various countries were coincidentally green-lit soon after his election, suggesting that perhaps some foreign governments were trying to curry favor with the new president through his business interests. The family of Trump's son-in-law and senior adviser, Jared Kushner, has touted the business opportunities that come from being tightly tied to the Trump administration. White House advisers have plugged Trump products in official appearances. Trump, who like most real estate developers finances many of his projects privately, is reportedly deep in debt to foreign creditors. Since he refuses to tell us, we don't know which ones; nor do we know how that debt has or will influence foreign policy. Worse still, the State Department is complicit in this cross-pollination between Trump's government and Trump's profits. In April 2017, ShareAmerica, a website run by the State Department, advertised Trump's Florida resort, going as far as to call Mar-a-Lago the "Winter White House."

As of this writing, more people on the right appear to be for opening what had been a pretty blind eye to these ethics issues. My hope is that we will continue to see more and more congressional Republicans insist on ethics standards and presidential (and presidential family) accountability. The Republican Party line that our nation should always come first is at odds with an executive branch that may be lining its own pockets first.

2. UPHOLD RELIGIOUS LIBERTY

Though I am a churchgoer, I am no saint, and I don't pretend to be. I attend services not because I am above sin but because I am not. We all have our faults and our flaws. That said, my religious beliefs do deeply inform my social consciousness, guiding me to fight for causes I believe in. Following my conscience is my deepest duty, and I take it very seriously. My ability to follow the social gospel depends on my right to religious freedom, and my commitment to defending this right is something I share with many conservatives.

This country was founded by religious believers who were persecuted for following an understanding of God that differed from that of the state-sanctioned Church. Building on this tradition, the founding fathers enshrined the right to religious liberty, making sure that the state could not establish a religion and force citizens to convert. Not only is this tyrannical, but it is impossible—no coercion or law can change a person's heart. While she might change her rituals and outward practices, her heart remains steadfast and her beliefs remain her own.

We protect religious liberty because your beliefs are yours; they are private, and you are free to draw on your private beliefs to guide your actions. The state does not impose religious practices on you, and you in turn do not impose religious practices on others via the state.

For years, I've spoken out against liberal attitudes that seem to be tolerant of everyone *except* the religious. For those who do not believe, it can be hard to understand the importance of being able to worship freely. I have been scoffed at by fellow liberals for believing. Conservatives, I've found, by and large accept that I can be both a political intellectual and a man of faith. Many of you come from the same background. You know that intelligent debate and rigorous critical thinking aren't hampered by spirituality or the study of sacred texts. Indeed, our political discussions are only sharpened by a consideration of perspectives and ideologies of all sorts. When we seek to preserve religious liberty, we do so because we recognize how critical it can be in deepening political views. For many people, religion provides the backbone for belief, community, and moral guidance, informing how we act and vote.

Of course, religion cannot be used as a license to discriminate. While the freedom to worship is a vital part of my and many Americans' lives, we must acknowledge an uncomfortable historical truth: This freedom has been extended selectively. Additionally, there is a long tradition of distorting religious tenets to justify beliefs and practices we now understand to be morally abominable, including the forced migration and genocide of indigenous people, the chattel slavery of Africans and their descendants, and legalized racial segregation.

Indigenous people who practiced religions our founding fathers did not understand were not considered equal. Instead, many early Americans cast indigenous Americans as "savages" or "heathen," creating a justification for stealing their land and decimating their traditions, customs, and communities. Native people were forcibly converted by settlers or were promised food and shelter in exchange for worshipping in a particular way.

Some Christians in the early 1800s believed that human slavery was ordained by God. Pro-slavery advocates in the American colonies used the Bible to justify their practices. In this interpretation of Christianity, slavery was recognized as God's plan—it was simply part of the way things were meant to be. Of course, abolitionists also appealed to the Bible to make their claims and in doing so were accused of attacking God's natural and ordained structure for human society.

In the Jim Crow era, Christianity was again used to defend racism. It was commonplace to hear pro-segregation preachers declare that God had separated the races and that to integrate them would be a great sin. None of this is new to the student of history, but the broader knowledge of how racism has consistently infiltrated and distorted Christianity has been lost to time. Over and over, religious doctrine has been used to grant moral authority to shameful, immoral acts.

The lesson here is not, as some liberals are quick to assume, that organized religion is evil. Nor is any of this history meant as an attack on Christianity. For me to do so would be to attack my own faith and family. My point is to remind us of how any faith can be bent and twisted into a shadow of itself—a force used to exclude and dominate rather than to liberate, inspire, and lift people up. Let this history serve to remind us that religion has been used to dismiss demands for equality. Today, some believers use religion to justify withholding equal rights from women and members of the LGBTQ community. They make claims about what is natural and ordained by God that perfectly parallel the claims made by defenders of slavery and members of the KKK who advocated for racial segregation. It was shaky moral ground to stand on in the past, and it's the same shaky ground now. I can only hope that conservatives, with your deep and appropriate wariness about human fallibility, will remember this history.

If you decide that some religions deserve more freedom to thrive than others, you make an opponent of those you exclude— Muslims like the Yousseffs, who share your values and need people like you to stand up for their commitments to family, faith, and individual responsibility. It would be morally consistent and politically wise for conservatives to embrace and defend folks from across all faiths who believe in strong families, personal discipline, work ethic, entrepreneurship, and educational attainment.

3. RESPECT ALL AMERICANS

Sometimes it feels to me as if conservatism today has been distorted to focus primarily on one group of people. So much of what now gets called "conservative" is really directed at helping straight white men, who are usually Christian. I have nothing against straight white Christian men—and indeed I reprimand liberals for their self-defeating demonization of this group. But if liberals unfairly condemn white men, conservatives disproportionately lionize them. Liberals can't blame white guys for every problem in the world, but conservatives need to stop thinking that white guys' problems are the only problems in the world.

Tribalism, in short, is at risk of taking down conservatism and perhaps America along with it. Millions of Americans of every race, ethnicity, income level, and gender might agree with your policies and proposals on paper; millions more hold personally conservative values. But a lot of right-wing rhetoric and actions chase away hordes of people who might otherwise resonate with most of your agenda. At best, you are leaving votes on the table; more often, you are driving them into the Democratic Party and energizing them against you. I don't mind that dynamic in the short term, because mistakes like that help Democrats maintain our big, blue, multiracial coalition. But over the long term, this arrangement is terrible for everyone—especially groups like African Americans, who vote 90+ percent for Democrats. When Republicans decide to just write off or forfeit whole groups, it lets Democrats take those same groups for granted. Liberals can win votes with rhetoric rather than results. When there is no real competition for black votes, African Americans are left with two bad choices: get run over by the Republican bus or be stuck in the back of the Democrats' bus, where we are expected to give massive support in exchange for pitiful outcomes. More competition might lead to better options.

Conversely, true conservatives should want to support citizens across communities, including socially conservative African Americans, LGBTQ individuals seeking legal marriage and adoption rights, women who hold down jobs while giving birth to and helping to raise our kids, and hardworking immigrants who often fill jobs that no other Americans will perform.

This might surprise you, but a lot of black people would probably be Republicans if the party were not so hostile and toxic. Look at the two strongest institutions in the African American community: the black church and the hip-hop community. The African American community is strongly oriented toward religious worship. Many vital services—daycare, education, care for the sick, and service to the poor—are organized through church communities. If you can get past the often vulgar lyrics, you will discover that hip-hop music fundamentally celebrates hard work, wealth creation, and entrepreneurship. We have been hustling since day one—it's what hip-hop music is all about. Many black voters embrace community, family, and respect for tradition—showing leadership in our churches, schools, civic associations, and workplaces.

But the Republican Party routinely fails to recognize or respect these facts—instead portraying African Americans in conservative media and political messaging as a dysfunctional community of criminals seeking handouts. This is sad but not surprising: Going back to Richard Nixon, some GOP leaders have cynically tried to win white votes by going after programs seen as aiding African Americans. At a human level, our social circles in America remain largely segregated by race. Negative media portrayals of African Americans add to suspicion and hostility. These dynamics combine and create ample opportunity for negative stereotypes to infect people's beliefs. This tendency is well documented and widespread—I see it every day when I talk to liberals who cartoonishly characterize all conservatives as heartless robber barons sitting on a pile of gold or ignorant redneck evangelicals who have no capacity for independent thought. These impressions are distortions rooted in stereotypes, and they are false on both sides.

The Republican Party's worst elements often inflate stereotypes and caricatures that go back centuries. Media personalities

on the conservative network Fox News have time and again ma-
ligned African American elected officials and community leaders.
Bill O'Reilly once deemed African Americans unfit for jobs because "they're ill-educated and have tattoos on their foreheads."
Tucker Carlson referred to black civil-rights leaders Al Sharpton
and Jesse Jackson as "hustlers and pimps." Even my friend Eric
Bolling once joked that Congresswoman Maxine Waters smokes
crack. It is not terribly surprising, then, that there is a correlation
between Fox News viewership and indicators of racial resentment
on surveys.

African Americans have heard this ugly stuff all our lives. Too
often, I hear right-wing pundits suggest that black folks vote Democrat because they are lazy and looking for a handout. They forget
that the vast majority of African Americans get up every morning
and go to work (unless they were on the overnight shift, in which
case they might sleep in). Not only do tens of millions of African
Americans work, we often do the worst jobs or hold down multiple
jobs, with low pay and inadequate benefits.

Of course, there are cases where citizens go unemployed for
long stretches of time because they lack skills or live in areas
where jobs aren't available. This problem doesn't hurt just African
Americans. Think back to Bryce Shoemaker, who has been out of
work for more than four years and whose son is struggling with
addiction issues. Commerce and jobs have dried up in his town,
but he cannot afford to move elsewhere or go back to school to get
trained in a trade that requires new skills. The same pattern holds
in many African American neighborhoods. Obviously there are
tough pockets of intergenerational poverty in both urban centers
and rural communities. But Republicans give away millions of
votes simply by repeatedly—overtly and subtly—portraying black
people as the face of poverty, crime, and dysfunction. When it
comes to the black vote, it seems the Republicans never miss an
opportunity—to miss an opportunity.

African American working-class folks and white working-class folks have a tremendous amount in common. Both parties should do more to offer opportunities for education and employment in the blighted pockets of our nation. Democrats have too often failed on both fronts, taking the black vote for granted and ignoring the needs of the white working class. These failures contributed greatly to Hillary Clinton's defeat, and they are a wake-up call to many of us. Republicans should wake up, too. As long as race prejudice is allowed to highjack conservatism, the party of Lincoln will never be the party of color-blind meritocracy, which it claims every day that it wants to be.

Another conservative value is the belief that the nuclear family, with parents committed to each other through marriage, is the essential building block of American stability and success. Marriage rates have declined in recent decades, but the divorce rate has skyrocketed. This worries conservatives. Additionally, there are thousands of children born each year to parents who cannot provide for them. Many conservatives have adopted children, because they believe strongly in the sanctity of life and in providing care for all God's children, not merely their own biological offspring. Conservatives frequently invoke the need to preserve the institution of marriage and nuclear family, as well as the moral importance of adoption.

There is one group in America that has fought tooth and nail for the sacrament of marriage and the needs of adopted kids: the LGBTQ community. Too often, conservatives look at lesbian, gay, bisexual, and transgender Americans and see them as the opponent. Instead, you might see them as one of the few communities still willing to fight for the concept of marriage. They are the biggest champions of the right to adopt and start a family. Some of you see this and have shown up to advocate for LGBTQ allies. When I talk with you one-on-one, you tell me about your friend or relative who came out and how you love them and have embraced them. Yet even in cases where you hold these personal convictions, you still stand behind candidates who openly condemn LGBTQ rights and work to discriminate against individuals fighting for the right to start a family. When you refuse to speak up in public, or when you vote for candidates who mock and threaten members of the LGBTQ community, you miss an opportunity to defend the institution of marriage and help kids in need get adopted.

Immigrants who come to this country to seek a better life believe more strongly in the American dream—in the promise of economic enterprise and hard work—than any group of citizens I know. Here are communities of people who, without complaint, do some of the hardest jobs in America. They serve with distinction in our military, putting their lives on the line to protect us. They pick fruit and vegetables for more than twelve hours per day in the hot sun and cold rain. They clean our businesses and restaurants while the rest of us are asleep. They care for our children, serving as role models, chefs, and educators for our kids while we are at work. They take care of our sick and elderly loved ones, patiently administering medication, carrying our aging parents to and from the bathroom, and making sure that they are getting the nourishment they need. They build buildings, fix homes, and repair cars. They bring irreplaceable knowledge and skills to our technology companies, filling roles that we cannot fill with our own citizens. Silicon Valley—and the computer I am using to write this book—would not exist without the zeal, ingenuity, and diligence of immigrant workers.

Most of the immigrants described above dream of a day when they can call themselves American citizens. In many cases, they have waited years and years to come here. In other cases, they are willing to risk their own lives—and the lives of their families— because they believe that America is the place where dreams come true and hard work is rewarded. If conservatives want allies to foster a rebirth of American patriotism, you need look no further than the immigrant communities that you have long stigmatized. Again, common ground is there for the taking.

Hard work comes in so many forms: in long hours in a coal mine, in the CEO who wakes up at 5:00 A.M. to check the business alerts, and in the teacher who volunteers to coach the debate club or form a math team—just to make sure her students are getting the best possible education. But a great deal of hard work goes unseen or unrecognized—the work of parents, and in particular of mothers. Many mothers work to bring home paychecks to help their family survive and then pull a full second shift as household managers, taking care of their families and helping them thrive. Fathers and husbands need to do their fair share, but our society should give women more respect, and our laws should protect them, not punish their choice to become mothers. Conservatives recognize the value of a parent who is dedicated to her child's growth, health, education, and well-being. During the first months of a child's life, a baby is wholly dependent on a parent for food, diaper changes, physical contact, and emotional support. We know that babies who receive good care from their parents fare much better for the rest of their lives. Yet we have inadequate laws in place to help families, especially families with working moms, give this essential care to their children. In many cases, mothers are forced to choose between earning a living and raising a child. A pro-family party worthy of the name would immediately pass laws to give American mothers and families more options. Fortunately, Ivanka Trump understands this issue and has become a champion for solutions. When the rest of the GOP follows her lead, the economy, the conservative movement, and (most important) our families will all be better off.

It is essential that conservatives do everything they can to stand up for the basic rights of women. They comprise 50 percent of the population and still face serious challenges. The current

President of the United States has not been the champion that they deserve. He openly admitted to committing crimes against women in the form of sexual assault. He has even bragged about kissing women and grabbing their genitalia without asking for consent. You'll remember what he said on tape, that he can do anything he wants to a woman he wants because he's a star. He gets away with it, all right, but not because he's a star. The fact that we as a society are too comfortable shrugging off women's pain and stories is what enables him—and men like him—to get away with their terrible behavior. In the age of Trump, women everywhere are reporting an uptick in rude and predatory behavior by men in the workplace and in public spaces. Republican defenders of law, order, and virtuous conduct need to be louder—not quieter—in times like these.

What might happen if conservatives made a real concerted effort to woo black voters, immigrant Americans, the LGBTQ community, and women? Our country would be better off for it. By dropping tribalism and instead hewing closer to your own values, conservatives would create real competition and elevate the debate. If both parties are competing for the support of these groups, it helps all of us. Underserved communities will finally have leaders striving harder to deliver. Politicians will be forced to turn to real solutions instead of blame and excuses. And the combined result will make America stronger.

4. FIX YOUR PARTY

If you look at the actual numbers, Republicans won control of the presidency and Congress in 2016 without winning the hearts and minds of the majority of Americans. It is a party built to win elections; now it is trying to govern a country—and it is struggling. In short, the Republicans took a shortcut to power through gerrymandering in 2010 and riding Donald Trump's coattails in 2016.

This speaks to a brokenness at the heart of the party, and it is a bad omen for the future of conservatives.

In May 2017, the Supreme Court handed down a decision that came as a shock to North Carolina Republicans. It declared that the congressional district maps, carefully drawn to give Republicans an advantage, were null and void. The reason? The court concluded that, despite protestations to the contrary, the maps were created using race as a predominant factor to draw their lines. The state government had cordoned black voters off into a tiny number of outrageously drawn districts spanning hundreds of miles, leaving the rest of the population spread across the remaining districts and giving Republicans a significant electoral advantage. If all the black voters are contained in one or two districts, after all, then they can't swing elections in any others. Rather than draw fair districts and compete for black votes—at the risk of possibly losing some seats in the short term—Republican Party operatives decided to write off all black voters and instead try to minimize their influence. The Supreme Court recognized this as an instance of intentional gerrymandering: when an election process is undermined due to district boundaries being manipulated in service to one party or class.

In addition to using gerrymandering, Republican politicians have also suppressed votes. Numerous states have passed laws requiring specific forms of photo identification to vote. This may seem like a benign, commonsense prerequisite, but we need to ask what problem this is trying to solve. Independent experts have found no evidence of in-person voter fraud widespread enough to have any impact on an election, identifying only rare one-off cases that made no difference to the electoral outcomes. There is certainly no evidence for the preposterous claims made by Trump that three million undocumented workers voted in the 2016 election. But nearly all experts agree that photo-identification laws do end up making it harder for Americans to vote; even so-called free

ID programs have costs associated with them, from taking time off work, to transportation costs, to associated fees for acquiring the documentation needed to get the ID in the first place.

Even if voter-ID laws pass muster with you, other Republican shenanigans will leave you shaking your head. In 2015, the state of Alabama shut down DMVs in thirty-one counties, including every county where black voters make up over 75 percent of the total registered voters. These ID-issuing office closures came on the heels of the voter-ID law, leaving those who did not already have identification with precious few and expensive options. Republican-controlled legislatures have also outlawed "early voting"—only after African Americans started taking advantage of those opportunities in large numbers.

I understand that conservatives are concerned about the integrity of elections. But conservatives should be just as skeptical when the state makes it harder to vote as they are when the state tries to make it harder to buy a gun. Both are cherished rights. I would also think that a conservative who respects democracy would want voters to pick their elected representatives, not the other way around. Yet, through gerrymandering, elected representatives can pick and choose their voters down to the household.

This gerrymandering is not in your long-term interest. Rather than building a hearts-and-minds majority in support of conservative values or its policy agenda, some powerful conservatives have focused on gaming the electoral system to contrive majorities where they shouldn't exist. If you continue down this path, it will backfire. We will come to a breaking point where a critical mass of people will decide that Republicans are more focused on control than on building a coalition that can govern. Such a strategy courts chaos.

Fortunately, sober-minded conservatives already know how to build a stronger and more representative Republican Party. Following the 2012 presidential loss, the Republican National Committee produced a report detailing why the party lost and what it needed to do to ensure long-term success. It made a number of recommendations—many of which are in line with my own outsider's advice. First, Republicans should embrace comprehensive immigration reform and end nativist language. Second, they concluded that harsh language and legislation targeting LGBTQ Americans hurt electorally. Third, they determined that Republicans were engaged in an echo chamber of belief—caused in part by choosing news sources like Fox News and only talking to colleagues and friends with similar beliefs—that resulted in a distorted understanding of the empirical reality of certain policies as well as voters' interests. Finally, the report warned that the Republican Party was at risk of becoming the party of rich white guys even as America was becoming browner, younger, and as inequality was growing. The report suggested reaching out to the populations I outlined above—people of color involved in faith communities, immigrants, LGBTQ folks focused on marriage and family, and women. Again, this analysis didn't come from me or from any liberal think tank. This was the Republican Party itself crunching the numbers and looking to the future.

What knocked your party off track? Two things. First of all, the party nominated Donald Trump, and he blew up basically every item on that list. Demonizing immigrants was the foundation of his campaign; he used dismissive language about "the blacks" and called black communities "hellholes." He picked a vice president with a long record of anti-gay advocacy. And, of course, Trump's entire public image is based on being a rich businessman. The question every conservative must ask is whether you really believe, in your heart of hearts, that Donald Trump is the future of conservatism. I know many of you do not.

I have talked to countless conservatives who feel apprehensive about or even hostile toward Trump. In the run-up to his election, a decent chunk of conservatives spoke out against his sexist boasting, his bigotry, and his ignorance. Yet at the end of the day, many thoughtful, compassionate conservatives held their nose and voted for Trump because they wanted to change the tax code or deregulate finance or ensure the appointment of a pro-life Supreme Court justice. Of course, voters across the board do not always agree with everything their candidates do and say, either; sometimes we have to vote for people we feel lukewarm about. But this election was different. Trump and his administration are different. What they stand for—and what they do—runs counter to the fundamental beliefs of millions of conservatives.

Now that Trump is in office, I have been saddened to see so little resistance from the many conservatives who spoke out against him. Where are these critical voices now?

The good news for you is this: The second thing you'll notice about that Republican-commissioned postmortem is that it says little about changing or giving up on traditional conservative values. It doesn't say that conservatives must drop their emphasis on faith, family, country, hard work, personal responsibility, local government, or entrepreneurship. You might need to change how you talk about those values. You will definitely be forced to understand how those values come to life in a modern age, in which we can't turn back the clock to the America of our youth. Families look different, faith looks different, and entrepreneurship does, too— but your values still give you a solid foundation to build on.

5. SOLVE REAL PROBLEMS

Conservatives can bring all these threads together by getting back to the core purpose of politics and public service: to solve America's real problems. You may say that conservatives are *already* trying to solve real problems. Hear me out. If you've been following along, you'll know that I think we mainly need better conservatives, not fewer of them.

There is a difference between a conservative party and an anti-liberal party. In recent years, the Republican Party has tried to bring many different constituencies together—Southern evangelicals, poor whites ignored by Democrats, rich bankers concerned with financial regulation, and many more. A good way of uniting otherwise disparate tribes is to pit them against someone—in this case, liberals. This has resulted in a party that is anti-liberal rather than pro-conservative. Starting in the nineties, Republicans built an army to win the culture wars. Now, having sacked Rome, they're facing tough problems. It is challenging to turn these incongruous and marauding troops into a policy-focused governing alliance, capable of and interested in getting things done.

This coalition is tenuously held together by a commitment *against* the liberal agenda and against liberals themselves. This means that blocking action by liberals, rather than working toward solutions, becomes the primary commitment. Think of Mitch McConnell's directive to his colleagues that their main goal should be to make Obama a one-term president. His legislative priorities were negative, not positive. Although he failed to achieve that goal, McConnell forged and led the most effective opposition party of the modern era. He successfully blocked action on climate change, any sort of infrastructure jobs package, middle-class tax cuts, and countless judges and executive-branch employees. He even managed to shrug off constitutional guidance and hundreds of years of precedent and declare that the sitting president would not be allowed to fulfill his constitutional responsibility to appoint a justice to the Supreme Court. Or consider recent congressional threats to shut down the government altogether, putting vital services and millions of jobs on the line, all in an effort to block Democratic legislation. These efforts were led by members of the congressional Freedom Caucus—associated with the Tea Party movement—who were sometimes willing to hold their party and the rest of the country hostage in order to stymie legislation.

I have heard numerous Republican friends and politicians bemoan this approach. I know that many of you are committed to the hard work of governing, and I want you to ask yourself: What do you owe to the people who are counting on you for a decent education, for access to jobs, for stable housing and a vibrant community? You have poor people in your party in red states and red counties. But you haven't done much for them. You accuse the Democrats of letting down our poor urban voters. But the modern conservative movement is structured to ignore its poor rural and suburban base in the same way. Sooner or later, your constituents will realize that you are not building anything, that you are not promoting their interests. In the short term, potshots at liberals and refusals to work on bipartisan legislation can curry favor with Republican activists and their media boosters. But at the end of the day, ordinary conservatives—maybe people like you—are being left behind.

Make a push to move your party from being anti-liberal to pro-conservative. There are big problems that could benefit from conservative policy ideas: criminal-justice reform, the opioid epidemic, keeping our air and planet free from harmful pollutants, creating new jobs and training opportunities for those left behind in the digital economy. These problems impact liberal and conservative citizens alike. Solving them requires us to put our heads together and put in some hard work.

Turning the Republican Party away from defeating liberals and toward solving real problems is smart politics. You have the opportunity to show your base that you can deliver on what you promise and to show potential new voters what you really stand for. There are so many examples of bipartisan success to draw on. Think of the extraordinary work done by conservative Senator Orrin Hatch and the late "liberal lion" Senator Ted Kennedy, who could not have disagreed more. As Orrin Hatch said when Kennedy died: "If the two of us—positioned as we were on opposite sides of the political spectrum—could find common ground, we had little trouble enlisting bipartisan support to pass critical legislation that benefited millions of Americans." Over the years, their legislative achievements were staggering. Together, they spearheaded the passage of the State Children's Health Insurance Program (CHIP) to provide health insurance to children of the working poor, provided tax credits to spur treatment of rare diseases, and improved the availability of care for low-income, uninsured, and underinsured victims of AIDS and their families. They passed the Americans with Disabilities Act. The list goes on and on. During this work, the two became close friends who deeply respected each other. They argued, laughed, cried, and—most important—legislated together for decades.

Working together in this way is not easy, but it is what our country desperately needs. In the end, the promise of America is liberty and justice for all. My fellow liberals are so focused on justice we too easily forget about liberty. Conservatives can be so committed to liberty that you become blind to cases where injustice curtails freedom. We need each other. We cannot improve this country alone.

If we focus only on winning elections, we end up demonizing the other side. If we focus on solving problems, we're forced to build bridges. To build bridges, we must listen to each other. When we listen to each other, both sides change and grow. We find ways to disagree without disrespecting each other. As we better articulate our visions and solutions, we find points of tension—but also points of cohesion. We are forced to defend our beliefs to people who disagree with us, which makes them stronger and reveals the cracks. This is what America needs, and it will take contributions from all of us to get to a better place.

CHAPTER FOUR

WHITELASH: MYTHS AND FACTS

In 2008, when Barack Obama was elected President of the United States, I sat on my sofa with friends and family in front of our TV, my four-year-old son in my lap. It was an emotional time for me—my father had passed away only months before. I missed him. And I wished so much that he could have seen this historic moment. Like most African Americans, we had doubted that we would ever see the election of a black president in our lifetimes. My parents were born under segregation. My twin sister, Angela, and I are ninth-generation Americans, but we were the very first people in our family to be born with all of our rights recognized by America's government. The ink was still drying on desegregation laws in the 1970s South, and courtroom battles to enforce them were still raging when we were little. My mother, whose prescribed inferiority as a black woman had been etched into law long before she was born, delivered this message daily: We could achieve anything we wanted to, because we were as smart and capable as any other kids. But we would have to work five times as hard as white children, because of the color of our skin. Both of our parents taught us that black excellence was the only sure weapon against racism; therefore, we were expected to do our absolute best at all times and in all situations. And yet I'm not sure I had dared to dream of what I was about to witness, sitting there on the sofa with my own son. Because of the hope Obama inspired in Americans—in red states and blue, among whites and blacks, ninth-generation Americans and first, student dreamers in the cities and working-class people in the heartland—the impossible had been accomplished. Like so many Americans, I was filled with joy and elation—and tremendous pride for my country.

Election night 2016 was not quite that way.

SITTING UNDER THE GLARING LIGHTS of the CNN set, thousands of miles from my wife and children, I watched my most dire predictions come true and my worst fears become reality. Sorrow overtook me. What was I going to tell my sons?

As my fellow pundits offered up their best takes, the situation seemed almost absurd. Our first round of topics was antiseptic and abstract: We were discussing votes and counties, turnout and stats. But I knew that in truth millions of people across the country were terrified and grieving. My phone was blowing up with concerned text messages from women and men, gay and straight, immigrants and born-and-bred Americans, Muslims and Jews, people I'd known for decades and others whom I had met only during the campaign. They all wrote with the same fears. My wife texted me about the boys, then eight and twelve; she was hoping that I might be able to reach out and comfort them. They were sad and scared, she said.

But we were on air, and I couldn't make phone calls from the set. I was going to have to try to address my own children—and speak up for all my friends—on live television, before tens of millions of people. I tried to gather my thoughts.

I pulled out a pen and wrote two words on my notepad. One word was "parents." The other word was "whitelash."

When it was my turn to speak again, I turned to my regular sparring partner, the conservative Jeffrey Lord. Over the past months, we had become the "Bert and Ernie" of political analysis. Ideologically, we disagreed passionately on just about everything, which made for good TV. But now was no time for fireworks. Jeffrey had believed in Trump all along. And now his team had won. Good grace and professionalism required that I congratulate him on his dark horse winning the race. I did so. Then I took a deep breath and spoke. To my friends. To my wife and our sons. And I think, in some small way, for my father.

It's hard to be a parent tonight, for a lot of us. You tell your kids, "Don't be a bully." You tell your kids, "Don't be a bigot." You tell your kids, "Do your homework and be prepared." And then you have this outcome. And you have people putting children to bed tonight, and they're afraid of breakfast. They're afraid of how do I explain this to my children.

I have Muslim friends who are texting me tonight saying, "Should I leave the country?" I have families of immigrants that are terrified tonight. This was many things. This was a rebellion against the elites. True, it was a complete reinvention of politics and polls. It's true. But it was also something else.

I thought one of the other commentators might jump in and interrupt me, but no one did. I still had the microphone, with a global audience numbering in the tens of millions. This was no time to duck, dodge, or flinch. Someone needed to address the elephant in the room—clearly and directly.

We've talked about everything but race tonight. We've talked about income, we've talked about class, we've talked about region. We haven't talked about race. This was a whitelash.

This was a whitelash against a changing country. It was a

whitelash against a black president, in part. And that's the part where the pain comes. And Donald Trump has a responsibility tonight to come out and reassure people that he is going to be the president of all the people who he insulted and offended and brushed aside.

The video clip of me saying those words, even as I fought back my own tears, was viewed tens of millions of times, all around the world. Many loved my commentary—especially parents who agreed with my assessment of the challenges of parenting at the dawn of the Trump era. Millions who saw the dark clouds of racial intolerance gathering throughout the Trump campaign felt affirmed. The nasty underside of the Trump campaign felt all-too-familiar to many African Americans of my parents' generation,* and they nodded in special recognition. For weeks after the election, people of all ethnic backgrounds came up to me on the streets, in airports, and in restaurants to shake my hand, snap a selfie, and thank me for expressing their truth in that moment. My comment had struck a chord with them.

But for millions of others, it struck a nerve. Many Trump voters deeply resented the term "whitelash." They thought that it tarred every single Trump voter as a bigot. Many Republican voters felt demeaned, disrespected, and dismissed. They were angry, even hurt. Some saw the term itself as racist; they asked what would have happened to them if they had called the election of Barack Obama a "black-lash." The right-wing media had a field day with it. A friend told me, "There seems to be a whitelash against the term 'whitelash.'" Her joke aside, it is true that my words offered comfort and clarity to people on one side of the

---

* In the wake of the civil-rights movement that dismantled Jim Crow segregation laws, Republicans developed what they called the Southern Strategy, which Richard Nixon popularized during his 1968 and 1972 campaigns. The Southern Strategy utilized a backlash method of bringing together Southern white conservative voters to realign the party. In effect, this racialized strategy galvanized white Southern voters.

partisan divide. And they created resentment, hurt feelings, and confusion for many on the other side. The fact that one man's election-night lament could provoke such opposite reactions, on such a massive scale, is telling in itself.

And yet here's the irony: *Both sides may have profoundly misunderstood what I was trying to convey that night.*

LIBERAL OUTRAGE AT TRUMP'S DIVISIVE rhetoric is well documented. For progressives, his comments insulting Mexican immigrants, Muslims, and African American communities placed him beyond the pale of civilized society. To many, anyone who voted for Trump is therefore an open bigot, a closeted bigot, or a willing enabler of bigotry. Their mantra in the weeks after the election was: "If you voted for a racist, you are a racist." (Ditto for sexism, able-ism, etc.) In their minds, the tiny white-supremacist "alt-right" movement mushroomed overnight to include 63 million people—because they see all 63 million of Trump's voters as morally indistinguishable from the KKK.

I must admit that I can sympathize with this reaction. I was beyond disgusted by Trump's rhetoric, and I think he disqualified himself on day one with his campaign-announcement speech—which falsely implied that the majority of Mexican immigrants are violent criminals. I was disappointed that more Americans did not reject him outright, on that basis alone.

But we must be careful not to let our anger overwhelm our analysis or let our disgust obscure the data. If some liberals took my election-night commentary to mean that I think every Trump voter is a racist, they misunderstood my point. I was trying to highlight a dangerous dynamic within his coalition; I was not trying to describe the motivation of every one of his voters.

Because those motives were often mixed. It turns out there were Trump voters who told pollsters that they were offended by his racial rhetoric but they voted for him anyway—because they wanted the Supreme Court to ban abortion. I have personally talked with pro-life/anti-abortion mothers who voted for Trump but who would never want their children to talk about women or people of color the way he does. I have met Trump supporters who own farms that rely on immigrant labor; they definitely don't want Trump to build a wall or deport Mexicans, but they voted for him in hopes of fewer regulations and lower taxes. I have met veterans who worked with Muslim translators overseas and passionately oppose Trump's Muslim ban; they voted against Hillary Clinton, fairly or unfairly, because of how they felt about her handling of the attack at Benghazi. Part of some voter behavior may be as simple as this: There were Republicans who held their noses and voted for Trump (in the same way that some progressives held their noses to vote for Hillary Clinton); they found his comments "distasteful, but not disqualifying"—in part because they were balancing other factors like those above.

I am thinking of people like the Seitz family in Ohio, whom I visited on my CNN show after the election. Scott Seitz and his three sons had all voted for Trump. Both Scott and his wife, De-rinda, had backed Obama twice previously. (She abstained from voting for either presidential candidate in 2016.) They were a solid, churchgoing family with strong ties to organized labor. The Seitz men were proud of their home, their work ethic, their country—and their vote.

Over dinner, we talked about everything from stereotypes about Trump supporters, to the moral ambiguity of the Clintons, to the fallout over Hillary's deleted emails. These were people who had thought carefully about their vote. Ultimately, Scott told me that his vote for Trump came down to economics. He said that blue-collar workers in the rust belt, like him, felt ignored and ne-glected by the Democrats. But what about Donald Trump's racially charged, anti-immigrant, and anti-Muslim rhetoric, I had to ask. Didn't voting for Trump condone this kind of bigoted hate speech?

Cameron, one of Scott and Derinda's sons, told me that he worked with a large number of minorities at his job as an addiction counselor. He denied the implication I made about Trump voters condoning racist attitudes. Then Scott jumped in and explained that "we hear [Trump's offensive statements], we crumple it up and throw it away." He said that Trump's controversial comments didn't affect the decisions he had to make to feed his family.

I understand where the Seitzes are coming from. I hear their pain, and I want to give voice to that. That's why I invited them on my show, because this is a point of view that liberals who watch CNN absolutely need to hear. But while I appreciated their candor, the conversation underscored for me the inability for Americans who aren't white Christians to simply "crumple it up and throw it away" when it comes to Trump's racially insensitive words and, worse, the legislative actions that back them up. There is privilege in being able to compartmentalize your family's economic needs and separate them in your mind from attacks based on race and religion. Working-class black Americans can't do that as easily. Immigrant families can't, either. Nor can Muslims.

As much as I want liberals to understand where blue-collar families like the Seitzes are coming from, I want Trump voters like them to broaden their political agenda to include real compassion for the pain experienced by Americans who are black and brown. I want them to understand that the impact of their choice has created a living hell for American Muslims living in fear, for Latino workers facing deportation (including Dreamers, who know no other country but America), for Native Americans fighting the imposition of leak-prone oil pipelines, for those Americans (disproportionately people of color) who will face longer prison sentences under the reignited drug war. Because I see the pain that the Trump administration is inflicting on people I love, I will continue to challenge his supporters' decision to vote for him.

But that said: Intentions do matter, and we have to be able to draw distinctions. Someone who voted for Trump out of party loyalty or fidelity to a single issue is not the same as a white nationalist who celebrated Trump's victory as a win for white supremacy. Trump's stoking of racial animosity was one factor, but not the only factor, in his victory. Liberals need to keep that in mind—lest we paint too many people with the wrong brush and push persuadable people deeper into Trump's arms.

RACE MATTERS

If I had to write a dictionary definition of the term today, it'd go something like this:

> Whitelash: a militant backlash, powered by white working-class voters, against both the economic and cultural consequences of neoliberal economic policy.

I know that's a mouthful, which is largely why you won't hear me spouting that explanation on TV or in polite company. But I want you to understand what I was getting at that night. The economic consequence of neoliberalism is that big corporations are growing in power; the cultural consequence of neoliberalism is that nonwhite, non-Christian people are growing in number. My definition identifies and categorizes those white working-class voters who are angry about both—many of whom supported Trump.

You might ask: Why would I focus on the "white" working classes? Most commentators simply talk about Trump's appeal to "working-class voters," "blue-collar voters," or "industrial Midwestern voters." Why would I interject a racial term like "white"? Am I deliberately trying to be racially divisive?

No. I am trying to be accurate. The media somehow seems to forget that all workers are not white. People of color make up an important part of the working class. And nonwhite workers overwhelmingly reject Trump and the ideas he represents—here, throughout Europe, and around the world. African American workers voted against him by nearly nine to one. A supermajority of Latino and Asian American workers oppose him, too. We can't talk about blue-collar workers without acknowledging that people of every color and all genders work in blue-collar jobs. The rise of Trump has exposed and deepened a sharp racial divide *within* the U.S. working class. And we see similar developments in Australia, New Zealand, Canada, and across Europe.

Why are nonwhite workers not joining this so-called working-class revolt? To gain a proper understanding—and deeper insight into the revolt itself—it helps to consider the thinking and writing of Frenchman Thomas Guénolé, a professor at the Paris Institute of Political Studies. In September 2016, Guénolé wrote a book whose title—*La Mondialisation Malheureuse*—roughly translates to mean "Unhappy Globalization." In it, he persuasively makes the argument that society is no longer bipolar but is instead now "quadripolar." In other words, "It is not one idea against another, but rather four opposing ideas." He goes on to explain that "Today, most rich democracies are focused on two highly divisive issues. The first is economic globalization. . . . The second highly divisive issue is minorities: immigrants and those who identify as LGBTQ."

Think of the new political reality he describes as a grid with four quadrants, like the one on the next page. The vertical axis defines one's embrace or rejection of the pro-corporate, neoliberal agenda. The horizontal axis defines one's relationship to multicultural, multiracial inclusion. Overlaying the two axes creates four quadrants. Choosing different language from Guénolé's, I call them liberal elitism, conservative elitism, left-wing populism, and right-wing populism. (I also would add an element to Guénolé's work. In my view, each of these camps has positive and negative features—a light side and a shadow side. All four of these quadrants have important gifts to offer the world. And all four of them have shadow sides that hurt it.)

The liberal elites embrace both multiculturalism and global corporations. (Think Hillary Clinton.) The conservative elites are less enthusiastic about multiculturalism, but they embrace the

FOUR-WAY POLITICS

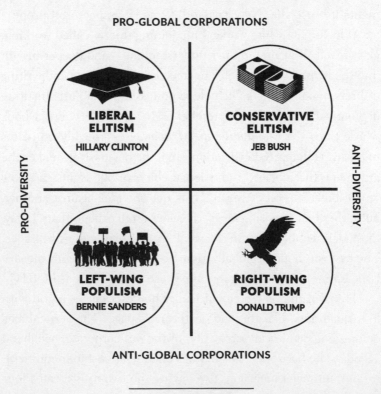

PRO-GLOBAL CORPORATIONS

PRO-DIVERSITY

ANTI-DIVERSITY

LIBERAL ELITISM
HILLARY CLINTON

CONSERVATIVE ELITISM
JEB BUSH

LEFT-WING POPULISM
BERNIE SANDERS

RIGHT-WING POPULISM
DONALD TRUMP

ANTI-GLOBAL CORPORATIONS

Hat tip to Thomas Guénolé

corporate agenda of free trade, low taxes, weak unions, and few regulations. (Think Jeb Bush.) The left-wing populists reject the elite corporate agenda, but they do embrace people of all colors, gender expressions, sexualities, and faiths. (Think Bernie Sanders or Elizabeth Warren.)

But the right-wing populists reject free flow of both capital and workers; they oppose both free trade and immigration, especially from non-European, non-Christian countries. (Think Donald Trump, especially under the influence of Steve Bannon.)

Trump supporters typically deny that his appeal is related in any way to some white voters' discomfort with America's changing demographics. But according to recent studies by the PRRI (Public Religion Research Institute) and *The Atlantic,* the feeling of identity threat, or racial dislocation, was more significant than even class in determining who voted for Donald Trump. And fears about immigration and "foreign" influence predominated. Forty-eight percent of white working-class voters echoed the sentiment that they felt like a "stranger in my own country." More than six out of ten white working-class voters believe America needs a strategy to protect against foreign influence. Those who shared that fear were 3.5 times more likely to vote for Trump than those who did not share their concerns. Other studies tell a similar tale.

These insights help us understand why Trump's movement appeals to white workers but repels nonwhite workers: Its anti-corporate message is marbled with rhetoric against diversity. Right-wing populists don't like corporations sending their jobs to foreign lands. They also don't like those foreign lands sending their workers here. Therefore, their message tends to favor native-born white Christian workers over all other workers. They also tend to defend the interests of heterosexual cisgendered male workers over the needs of women in the workplace and/or LGBTQ workers.

As a result, nonwhite, non-Christian, and nontraditional workers tend to stay away—leaving perfect conditions for white racial extremists to set up shop. If we don't acknowledge that fact and shine a spotlight on the dangers, evil can flourish in the dark. This is the threat to which I was trying to alert the country on election night. And it remains my greatest fear.

Let me be clear: There are right-wing populists who are simply strong patriots. They embrace traditional conservative values and are less comfortable than I am with multiculturalism. I disagree with them on many issues, but I do not see them as a threat to democracy. After all, reasonable people can disagree about trade policy, traditional gender roles, the risks and rewards of multiculturalism, or ideal immigration rates.

The problem is that otherwise respectable right-wingers are allowing something sinister to grow up in their midst, without acknowledging it—and without aggressively countering it. Taking up residence in the party of Lincoln today are overt neo-Nazis, white nationalists, and white supremacists. They traffic in hatemongering and even violence. They are growing in number and confidence. Militants on the angriest edge of right-wing populism are deliberately fanning the flames of racial fear and resentment; they are consciously trying to stoke, sustain, and intensify the whitelash—with racist reasoning, violent tactics, and authoritarian goals that would appall the vast majority of conservatives. As a result, we see the rise of what I call the "dirty right." (I don't want to dress it up as the "alt-right" or link it to legitimate conservative causes by calling it the "far right.")

Liberals must accept that every Trump voter is not a white supremacist. But conservatives should be worried that so many white supremacists are Trump voters.

The rise of the dirty right poses unique threats to individual safety, to conservatism's future, and to a free and inclusive democracy. To make matters worse, Trump has too often flirted with it. His former aide Steve Bannon is both a champion and a product of the dirty right. And others on the right have been too quiet about its growth and the dangers it poses. One need not be a liberal to be alarmed by these developments. Every American should be alarmed.

Consider these few examples of the onslaught facing our most vulnerable citizens:

In November 2016: At the University of New Mexico, a white male student wearing a Trump shirt attempts to rip the hijab—the head scarf that some Muslim women choose to wear in public—off a seventeen-year-old freshman. In Washington, D.C., a group of young white men physically assault a Guatemalan immigrant in order to "make America white again." In Indiana, a historically black church is vandalized with the words: Kill All Koons. In Queens, New York, a white middle-aged couple demands that a woman on the bus "take that disgusting piece of cloth off," before forcefully attempting to remove her hijab. A week before the election, a historic black church in Greenville, Mississippi, is set on fire, its walls spray-painted with the slogan "Vote Trump." In February 2017, volunteers scrub away racial slurs spray-painted onto the Tarbiya Institute mosque in Roseville, California. The words "Muslim Out" and further expletives about Allah and Islam drip down the stone walls of the building. Around this time, several Jewish journalists are sent photoshopped images of themselves being hacked apart by a Gestapo-clad Pepe the Frog.* On June 1, 2017, a noose swings in the segregation section of the Smithsonian's National Museum of African American History and Culture in Washington, D.C. On this same day, in Los Angeles, someone paints the N-word on NBA MVP LeBron James's fence.

Some in the right-wing media have reacted defensively, suggesting that the majority of these incidents are fraudulent and

---

* Pepe the Frog was a harmless cartoon associated with typical frat-boy culture— playing video games, smoking pot, eating pizza—in 2008. Over the course of many years, Pepe evolved into a symbol of hate, his smug expression the perfect canvas for racial invective and Hitler costume changes. Now recognized by the Anti-Defamation League as a hate symbol, Pepe's use on sites like 4chan, Reddit, Imgur, and Tumblr promotes racist, anti-Semitic, misogynist, and anti-LGBTQ sentiments.

even trying to discredit the Southern Poverty Law Center, which tracks hate groups and successfully sued the Ku Klux Klan. But in the days following the election alone, there were nine hundred reports of harassment and intimidation across the nation, according to the Southern Poverty Law Center. In the months since, hate crimes against African American, Muslim, Jewish, LGBTQ, Latino, and other groups continue to far exceed normal incident levels. White supremacist sites such as 4chan incubate vicious levels of harassment toward marginalized groups, often using Trump's subtweets as fodder. The FBI reported in December 2016 that twice as many hate crimes were being recorded in New York City. Daily, a rising number of abusive and violent racist attacks occur in American K–12 schools and universities, in churches and mosques, at the workplace, in grocery stores. These incidents would be disturbing enough if they were occurring only at the grassroots level. Unfortunately, the President of the United States has elevated white supremacist groups* via his Twitter platform and White House appointments, and he refuses to strongly condemn racist attacks. That's wrong. As I said in the "Open Letter to Conservatives," it is likewise wrong for the Republican Party to not loudly denounce the white-supremacist rhetoric or the empowerment of racists elements within the conservative ranks. Instead, too many turn a blind eye and pretend it's not happening, or refuse to mark its relationship to Trump's rise. Meanwhile, the bloody evidence continues to mount. On the one hand, good conservatives take great offense at being tarred with the same brush

---

* During Donald Trump's campaign, he encouraged his supporters to "knock the crap out of" protestors—often black protestors. In fact, Trump himself said he would cover the legal costs at a rally in Louisville, Kentucky, a promise he would later rescind when white supremacist Matthew Heimbach faced an assault-and-battery suit. What's more, the Ku Klux Klan has been emboldened by Trump. Will Quigg, KKK's California Grand Dragon, told 60 Minutes, "With Donald Trump as our president, it has given the white people, especially the white Christian people, a voice." Pastor Thomas Robb, a KKK member, said that Donald Trump's election has given white people "the courage to be more bold," and Robb's daughter, Rachel Pendergraft, also a KKK member, confirmed, "He helped legitimize this message."

as Steve Bannon, Sean Urbanski, Jeremy Christian, and Dylann Roof. On the other hand, however, they make no moves to quell a nasty tide rising within their own ranks. It's hard to see why they should have it both ways.

MY DESIRE TO FIND compassion for all sides comes from a personal place. Let me share a few more stories with you.

I had a job as a high school student in Tennessee, at *The Jackson Sun,* my local newspaper. I wanted to write, but because I was just a kid, they had me doing things like sorting the mail, inking the presses, stuffing inserts into the Sunday edition, moving bundles on and off the belt. That was my job all during senior year. The journalists had their desks in the front of the building, but manual laborers like me came and left through the back door.

Many of my co-workers in the back room of the *Sun* were beefy white guys in their teens and their twenties. A few were older. They operated the presses and all the machinery. They were working-class sons of the South who loved to hunt, fish, and tinker with their sports cars on the weekends. Their opinions on race were as rude and crude as you could imagine; we had many a shouting match—some friendly, some not—over the roar and clank of the machines. But they were the kind of "good old boys" who would pull over in the rain to help a stranger on the side of the road—no matter what color the stranded person was. And we shared a kind of workplace solidarity, born of our shared experience. We all entered the building through the back door together. We all would get covered in the same brown dust and black ink. At two in the morning, we all would finally get to go home and take a shower. (There was no point in showering before work.) Then I would eat whatever my parents had left for me on the stove and collapse into bed. I imagine they did the same.

This was in the 1980s, when public universities in the South were still struggling to get fully integrated. I was able to get a minority scholarship to attend the University of Tennessee at Martin, about an hour up the road. I signed up for entry-level journalism classes right away. Because of those same desegregation efforts, newspapers in the South had special internships for minority students. I was awarded one. That next summer I was back at the *Sun* again. But now I wasn't coming in through the back door, and I didn't work with the machines. I walked in through the building's front door, and I worked at a computer console with the other writers and the people in charge of the paper. Like all white-collar workers, I now showered *before* going to work.

That's a big, big difference in a small town. Over the next two summers, I saw some of the guys I knew from before. A few did head off to college or trade school. But a good handful of them were still there. They teased me and called me "College Boy," but I could tell they were proud of me. Maybe they were a little jealous, too. I don't know.

During my first summer, the management at the *Sun* started talking about upgrading their printing press. There was a lot of excitement about how the operations would improve with these new machines, which were on the cutting edge of automation. All of us were excited—the guys in the back most of all. Working at the *Sun* was no jumping-off place for them—it was their livelihood. They were proud of that paper and proud of their role in it.

And you know what happened? When the new press was completed, it was the size of a building. We all stood around and admired it. We applauded it. And soon after, most of the guys in the back got fired. Those workers were no longer needed, because the new press was almost fully automated.

When I heard about the layoffs, I felt a strange pang—of both compassion and foreboding. Here I was—someone who used to be in the same position—now on my way to a more secure career, thanks to a full scholarship and a minority internship. I was on a trajectory that would have been almost unimaginable for a young black man from Tennessee just a decade before. I was proud, in part because I knew the brutal racist history that African Americans had overcome to get scholarships and internships like that in place. I understood the deadly struggle waged by black and white civil-rights workers to open those doors for me. Besides, a four-year scholarship to a modest public university was not exactly fair compensation for nine generations of slavery and segregation. So I didn't feel guilty about my opportunities.

But I did feel empathy for my old buddies who'd lost their jobs.

And even then I had a concern that this was a perfect formula to create resentment and an eventual backlash. Allow mass displacement of white workers. Have no real plan to replace those jobs. Then highlight a few token efforts that help a tiny handful of people of color. It is easy to understand how some of my white co-workers might have seen the programs that helped me as a form of unfair discrimination against regular white guys like them. I can understand, on a human level, why some might resent the progress made by a handful of African Americans. Change is never easy, for any of us. Just step into an African American community experiencing the arrival of a new set of immigrant neighbors, and you'll see that prejudiced comments and attitudes aren't the purview of white folks alone. Some white working folks might understandably see someone like Barack Obama successfully ascend to the presidency, hear about a movement where people are crying out "Black lives matter," or read about a special program that funds mentoring for black boys, and think: "What about me? What about the ordinary white American family? Who's looking out for us?" It

wouldn't be the first time that black progress triggered white resentment.*

Donald Trump capitalized on those volatile emotions during
his campaign. As an outsider to the D.C. establishment, he positioned himself as someone who was carefully listening to the concerns of the white community, especially the working class. Trump
doubled down on his white Christian voters with promises to
make America great again by building a literal wall against Mexican immigrants and making blanket anti-Muslim statements left
and right.

Whenever white workers see economic progress stall and demographic change accelerate, the potential for racially coded
backlash politics is always present. It is not new, and it is not jus-
tifiable, especially in its most virulent, racist forms. But it is
understandable—and it is preventable. If we work to address people's legitimate economic concerns, it follows that they will be less
vulnerable to politics of fear and anger. Until those conditions are
addressed, aspects of the otherwise righteous protest movement
against the elite will continue to be co-opted by the more bigoted
and dangerous forms of populism.

Most people want to believe that they can treat everyone absolutely fairly, including people of other races. In polite company,
every decent American dutifully insists that he or she is "color-
blind"—ignoring skin color completely, in every life decision. To
admit otherwise would be to confess to the mortal sin of racism—
and risk being branded as such and possibly banished forever.

Yet studies, statistics, and even brain scans reveal that—
consciously and unconsciously—Americans still rely on snap judg-
ments and stereotypes, usually to the detriment of nonwhite

---

* During Reconstruction in the nineteenth century, black men and women who were
former slaves now seeking paid employment were suddenly seen as competition by
white workers, especially poor whites. By the turn of the century, Jim Crow laws were
being enacted to protect white economic interests, using race as a factor to segregate
black Americans and block them from gaining more political and economic freedoms.

people. Something significant is still going on in the American soul and psyche. But we can't easily talk about it. This conundrum creates a backdrop of tension and anxiety for most discussions about race in America—and that's even before you add in a character as explosive as Donald Trump.

WHERE DO WE FIND THE moral conviction to deal honestly with our changes and challenges? How do we find deeper reservoirs of hope and goodwill, of forgiveness and patience, in a nation as diverse and divided as our own? How do we find the strength to move away from confrontation and toward community—without soft-pedaling difficult facts and painful truths?

We might take some lessons from Charleston, South Carolina, and that community's inspiring response to the horrific mass murder of nine Christians as they prayed in church.

At the Emanuel AME Church in Charleston, South Carolina, on June 17, 2015, Dylann Roof, a self-proclaimed white supremacist, opened fire inside that historic black church in hope of inciting a "race war." Those horrifying murders show what happens when racial hatred is allowed to flourish unchecked.

I went to Charleston shortly after the murders. I was there with other CNN contributors; we were set up across the street from the church. It was so hot that we all kept sweating through our shirts. CNN crew members surrounded us with fans, and they let us seek refuge in air-conditioned vans during long commercial breaks, but nothing worked. We sat there under the bright lights on the sweltering raised stage, feeding our blood to the mosquitos and suffering.

But the heat outdoors was minor compared to the rage burning inside me. How was it possible for this young white man to go into a church, sit beside fellow churchgoers, pray with them, and then gun them down? It was our job to offer some sort of explanation to viewers, but I found myself inadequate to the task.

And it was not the first time. I was growing weary of trying to explain black tragedies on national television. I had been on the ground in Ferguson, Missouri, the year prior, covering the protests that followed the police killing of Michael Brown in that town. I got tear-gassed on camera, while trying to give my commentary on the tragic events there.

Whatever you think of the specifics of the Brown case, it has proven to be just one of many. In a few short years, a seemingly endless train of unarmed black bodies—Sandra Bland, Trayvon Martin, Tamir Rice, Philando Castile*, Keith Lamont Scott, Freddie Gray, Terence Crutcher, Eric Garner, and all too many more—have continued to fill our morgues, their lives taken by law-enforcement officials or vigilantes. With gang violence also flaring in cities like Chicago, a whole generation of African Americans has seemed to be getting crushed between unlawful street violence and unlawful police violence. The young activists who formed Black Lives Matter have used the only weapons they have—their bodies and their mouths—to stand for justice. But conservatives and Republicans—and a shameful number of Democrats, too—have roundly condemned them. Some in the media have seemed more concerned about the name of the protest group ("but don't all lives matter?") than about the killings that sparked the protests. It was then and still is incredibly frustrating.

What happened in Charleston, however, was a new low.

It would have been easy to brush Dylann Roof aside as one lone nut. But I knew better. White nationalist groups were and are on the rise; they had been growing in strength and numbers

---

* As I finalize the pages of this book, my phone alerts me that the cop responsible for the murder of Philando Castile, the unarmed black man whose murder was broadcast on Facebook Live by his brave and terrified girlfriend, was acquitted of all charges. Castile, when he was pulled over in his car, told the cop he was reaching for his wallet. He was shot and killed anyway—and the cop who murdered him was cleared of all charges. Castile's family left the courtroom barely able to hold themselves up, so heavy was their grief. Castile is remembered by the students at the Montessori school where he worked as a cafeteria worker and was beloved by all.

throughout the Obama years. As much as the mainstream media likes to shrug off black and Jewish concerns about white supremacist groups, the most serious terrorist threats inside the United States do not come from radical Islamists. They come from radical white extremists. According to *The New York Times,* Americans are seven times more likely to be killed by a white right-wing extremist than we are to be killed by an Islamist jihadist.

During that stifling day in Charleston, all these people kept milling about. Mostly black people, but a good number of white folks, as well. All of them looked bewildered, hurt. When I got done with my on-air commentary, it was beginning to get dark outside. A black police officer came over to my fellow CNN personality, Don Lemon, and me. "Hey, brothers," he said, "I want to show you something." He led us across the street to the church. It was cordoned off, but he got Don and me through the police lines. We went down the stairs and into the basement, where Roof had opened fire.

The blood had been wiped clean. The bodies were gone. We saw pictures of Jesus, inspirational slogans, big calendars of upcoming trips and activities. Crayon drawings of all the things that had been in the imaginations of the children who had been here just days before. The basement was a cared-for and well-to-do space. It was hard not to be impressed with how beautiful it was. Almost immaculate.

Except for the bullet holes in the walls.

The officer led us around and explained what had happened. How these people had been shot over here and those people had been shot over there. It felt surreal, to be standing in the very spot where human beings had lost their lives so senselessly. I turned to go after this macabre tour, but the officer said, "No, come on back here. I want you to see something else."

We kept walking through the basement, past more bullet holes, toward what would have been the back exit. A short flight of stairs led back up to the street level, a shattered glass door, more police tape. The officer pointed to the ground. At the foot of the stairs, the marble tiles lay broken and cracked. "Oh my God," I thought, "the weight of the bodies on the stretchers must have cracked the marble when they brought the victims out." I didn't want to see any more. I thanked the officer and turned to go again, but the officer asked me, "You know what that is?"

"The gurneys broke the tile?" I offered.

"No, no," he said. "This is where the last person fell, while trying to get out. The shooter kept firing down—and the bullets broke up the floor."

That's when I lost it. Some innocent churchgoer—like the ones I had met at innumerable conferences I had attended as a child with my grandfather—had gotten this far, a few steps away from safety, but had been shot again and again by a despicable racist. This coward. Rage and sorrow overwhelmed me. If I could have found the shooter at that moment, I might have strangled him with my bare hands. I wanted to pull a thunderbolt from the sky and strike him down. In that moment, I didn't feel very much Christian compassion or love. Maybe none at all.

The next morning, I was still seething. I could barely make eye contact with anyone. I was sitting with CNN anchor Jake Tapper, preparing to go on the air. We were both mic'd up, sweating, and sad. The funeral service was just beginning.

Suddenly we started to hear something—music, coming from across the street, from the church, Mother Emanuel. A big, beautiful, upbeat sound with drums and organ and piano. A chorus of voices, a soaring harmony. Totally discordant with how we were feeling. The camera people began saying, "What is that?" The music swelled around us. It seemed to lift us all from below.

"It's amazing," Jake said to me, off air. "How is it possible? They actually sound happy."

I smiled a little and sat up.

"That's not happiness," I told him. I explained that there is a distinction in the black church between happiness and joy. Happiness is dependent on external circumstances, but joy comes from within. Despite the circumstances, we say, "Hallelujah, anyhow." It's our way of saying that you're not going to take away my dignity or my inner knowledge that I have worth, if only in the eyes of my Creator. You're not going to take my humanity. You're not going to turn me into something other than a beautiful child of God.

The songs kept pouring out into the streets, which were filling up with people. Black people and white people, together. Many of them held each other and cried. The music reached out to all of us. It was a celebration and acknowledgment that the Charleston community could find a sense of deeper purpose and community, even in the face of the worst kind of racial violence. The capacity for forgiveness shown by the families of the victims toward Dylann Roof stands as a model of the most courageous, spiritually centered, and morally grounded response to hatred in our nation. The courts sentenced Roof to death, but family members say they do not want the killer to be killed in their name.

Even in the midst of division and despair, Charleston reminds me that human beings have untapped potential for forgiveness, solidarity, and transcendence. The black community has been forced to develop those resources and refine them over painful decades and centuries. The same can be said of other groups who have had to struggle to find a place in America. It is unfair that people suffering at the bottom and margins of our society are always expected to bear the burden of also being morally strong. America should not take such dignity and beauty for granted. The only fair response is for the rest of America to match the example set in that beautiful Southern town.

Understanding across all of these barriers of color and creed may sometimes seem impossible. But if the good people of Charleston can find that reservoir within themselves, find hallelujah, anyhow—then so can the rest of us.

As I ARGUED IN MY "Open Letter to Liberals," Americans on all sides need to be aware of the dangers of knee-jerk reactions and the needless polarizations to which they lead. Sometimes, in our human desire to ease discomfort, we turn toward the most expedient feel-good strategy—and away from solutions that will ultimately serve us. Frustration and resentment can be instruments for change, but they also make us vulnerable to divisive tactics. A multiracial democracy cannot function if tribalism takes over.

D.C. will continue to be a circus for a long time to come. The strength to rescue democracy and solve real problems will emerge from ordinary people. "Bipartisanship from above" served the global elite and divided the people. Today our political world is no longer bipolar but quadripolar. Each of the four poles has positive and negative features.

But right-wing populism's negative aspects—including authoritarianism, white supremacy, and violence—pose an unacceptable threat to democratic society. I have accused some politicians (including Trump) of flirting with fringe elements and deliberately stoking a form of "whitelash politics." All pro-democracy forces—from liberal to conservative—have an interest in blocking the rise of a violent, racist, and anti-democratic movement which appears to be growing on the right.

As a compelling alternative, we need a solution-oriented, positive populism. To be authentic, it must reflect a "bipartisanship from below," not above. That kind of breakthrough is possible, but only if dedicated Americans from all political traditions join forces to confront the acute pain in our society: the poverty, the broken justice system, the addiction crises—to name a few.

We all have work to do. On the left, we must challenge the class elitism and condescension that undermine our own causes. On the right, leaders must challenge the xenophobia and extremism that are ruining theirs. Both must stop sidelining women. And all must prioritize the needs of Americans—of all faiths and colors, in both red states and blue states—who are losing their lives and livelihoods under the present economic order.

Now we will explore ways to do so.

CHAPTER FIVE

PRINCE, NEWT, AND THE WAY FORWARD

Portraits in Strange Bedfellows

THE SCHOLARSHIP I RECEIVED TO ATTEND THE UNIVERSITY of Tennessee at Martin was a golden opportunity to get on track to become a professional journalist. And at no expense to my parents, to boot. It felt like a gift from above, and I vowed to make the most of it. As a sophomore, though, I found myself in the worst trouble of my young life.

At UTM, I helped to launch an independent student newspaper called *The Fourteenth Circle*. It was an exciting project that was in line with my ambitions to make change in the world. On the morning in question, my student peers and I had been feeling particularly pleased with ourselves. Full of bravado, we had just written, edited, and distributed the first edition. We had done the interviews, written the articles, taken the photographs, and drawn the cartoons. To support our endeavor, we sold the ads to local businesses. We knew without a doubt that through the sheer force of our prose alone, our paper would transform the UTM campus. We were so proud.

Unfortunately, our manifesto, which called for such radical changes as improving the cafeteria food and allowing opposite-sex visitation in the freshman dorms, was also in clear and indefensible violation of the Student Code of Conduct.

When the administration saw that first issue, we were dragged into the dean's office. There we sat, a bunch of maverick wannabes with our heads down, braced for punishment. We were given an ultimatum. We all had to agree to stop publishing the paper—or withdraw from the university.

As one of the editors, I was ready to stand for justice. Full of righteous fury, I squared my shoulders and looked the dean in the eye. "Fine. I'll withdraw. I don't want to be enrolled at a school that treats students this badly, anyway!" I stormed out of his office, slamming the door behind me.

But as soon as I got outside onto the quad, I crapped my pants at the thought of what my father would say. Here I was, squandering the college scholarship that had put me on the other side of the printing press in the first place. What would he say if he knew I got kicked out of school because of my cutting-edge food-court principles? *"Rah-rah roast beef"?*

I wasn't sure what to do. So I sought out the man I respected most on the Martin campus. Dr. E. Jerald Ogg, Jr., was a new journalism teacher—young, popular, and whip smart. He also happened to be a lawyer. If he was willing to defend me, I might have a chance. But if he sided with the dean—his boss—and agreed that we were out of line for publishing our own underground newspaper, I would have no choice but to withdraw from school.

I sat in his office as Ogg looked at the paper for a long time with an inscrutable expression. His eyes lingered over the more controversial articles. Finally, he looked up.

"There is no question that this paper is in direct violation of our Student Code of Conduct." He looked over his glasses at me severely, and his tone was solemn. Cringing inside, I met his gaze.

"The Student Code of Conduct is real important here at Martin," he continued. "It's one of our most sacred documents."

Here it came. The ax.

"But the First Amendment is more important," Ogg said. "And you are within your rights to publish anything you want in this country. You just need to do a better job of making it clear to your readers and your advertisers that this is not an official university publication." Reaching for the phone, he said, "Let me see what I can do."

Ogg worked with other professors to keep us from getting expelled. I kept my scholarship. And we continued to publish the paper, off and on, until the week I graduated.

YOU MIGHT BE INTERESTED TO know that Dr. E. Jerald Ogg, Jr., is a white, conservative Republican. I am not. But he was my first mentor, and to this day he remains one of my most trusted advisers.

It might seem unlikely that someone like me—a young progressive entering into the hotheaded phase of my lefty-est years—would come to admire, love, and trust a GOP mentor. But then again, I am my father's son. I often watched the evening news on the couch with my father, and listened intently to his explanations and opinions. He had a first-class bullshit detector and he interjected with perfectly timed, rapid-fire political critique throughout every broadcast. He would have made a hell of a pundit. In his eyes, a good man was a good man—and a no-good man was a no-good man—no matter what he looked like, where he prayed, or how he voted.

If my dad's sofa was my first university, Ogg's classroom gave me a virtual PhD in politics, journalism, and life. Ogg had the kind of background that was highly regarded by American conservatives and academics alike: A revered alumnus of UT Martin, he had been editor of the official student newspaper, earned a law degree someplace else, served as an active-duty judge advocate (JAG) in the U.S. Air Force, and then returned to the communications department as a faculty member. He is a good Christian man and a son of the South. Apart from more-obvious physical differences, he and my father shared a lot in common. They were both in the air force; they were both plainspoken and direct; and, most important to me, absolutely nothing could shake their commitment to instilling good values and a strong work ethic in the next generation.

The first time I entered Ogg's office, I'll admit, I almost turned around and left. A large framed photo of Ogg and none other than then–Vice President George H. W. Bush hung directly opposite the door. Ogg looked dignified and proud. With my left-wing politics, I couldn't imagine a more unlikely mentor than the man in the photo. I had to wonder if someone with his political beliefs would be for me—or against me.

But again and again, Ogg went above the call of duty to assure me that, despite our differences, he was *for* me. As a mentor, a professor, an intellectual, a friend—as a human being. In one of the hundreds of times I sat in his office, he told me something I would never forget. In his soft-spoken way, he told me that we had "different politics of the head but the same politics of the heart." He meant that the two of us cared about the same things; we just had different philosophies when it came time to act on those concerns. This notion has stuck with me my whole life—that good and decent people can disagree politically without disrespecting or even disliking each other personally. My relationship with Ogg remains the best example and proof of this point in my own life.

There is another photo—this one in my digital archives—that I return to every now and again. It shows Ogg with five journalism students: four women and me. I had finally become the editor of the official student newspaper, and Ogg was right there as the paper's faculty adviser. Since it was the eighties, we look confidently goofy—wide shoulders, wider hair. Ogg has a gentle, intelligent expression. We do, too. The photo always reminds me of a Benjamin Franklin quote: "Tell me and I forget, teach me and I may remember, involve me and I learn." It's the right sentiment for my formative years with Ogg. He believed in my talent, and I believed in his teaching. I took every class he taught. In my front-row seat to the right of his lectern, I asked every question I could think to ask.

Nonetheless, at one point I had decided that I wanted to transfer to Vanderbilt University. My girlfriend, a beautiful and brainy pre-med student named Monica Peek, was already enrolled there. I could see how many opportunities her prestigious university offered that were missing at my humble state university. Now that I knew what I was missing, it seemed logical to head off to better pastures.

In that office I knew like the back of my hand, Ogg confirmed that I had what it took to make it at a school like Vanderbilt. "Yes, you *could* go anywhere," he said. "But don't overlook what you have right here. None of our professors are famous academics. We hire tough retired journalists who wrote real stories, on real deadlines, in the real world. They are here to pass along everything they know to the next generation. There's no substitute for that. You get to absorb everything they learned in the field. If you take advantage of every other opportunity on this campus, you can go anywhere in the world from right here. But you will leave here with real skills, and you will have been nurtured by a faculty that really cares about you."

In his gentle but firm way, Ogg was telling me to see my rural roots not as a launching pad but as my home base. And he was teaching me to never dismiss the value of hardworking people in humble places. It was an important lesson.

He was right then, and he's more right now. I stayed at the University of Tennessee.

NELSON MANDELA HAS A LOT to say about knowing thy enemy. When a man who went from being a prisoner of his country to becoming its president says something, you should take him at his word. According to Mandela, "If you want to make peace with your enemy, you have to work with your enemy. Then he becomes your partner." My own journey has taught me this truth again and again.

Which brings me to Newt Gingrich, a man whom I met at CNN and from whom I've learned plenty. Many have wrinkled their brows at our friendship, but no one was more surprised than Newt Gingrich himself.

People forget that in 1994, the Democrats lost control of the U.S. House of Representatives in a historic wave election. The Democrats had held the majority in the House throughout my lifetime up until that point. Hell, not even in my parents' lifetime had the Republicans wrested power from the Democrats. But Bill Clinton's midterm-election losses—and the Republicans' seat gains—were staggering. Newt Gingrich, the new Republican Speaker of the House, was at the helm of that effort.

I immediately got every article and book that I could find by and about Newt Gingrich. I studied him very carefully. I disagreed with his policy agenda, made famous as his "Contract with America." But I wanted to understand the mind that had engineered a political upset of such spectacular proportions. I learned that, long before the 1994 midterm election, Newt had cleverly invested in fax machines and satellite television—cutting-edge technology at the time—so he could arm his troops with the best sound bites and arguments. Republican candidates listened to his speeches on audiocassettes as they drove around to give talks of their own. He had boiled his messaging theory down into a single document called "Language: A Key Mechanism of Control." I also learned that he had systematized his worldview into an entire educational curriculum called *Renewing American Civilization*. I eventually got my own copies of those lectures on audiotape.

That's when I knew that progressives were in trouble. At first, many liberals assumed that Newt's entire movement was just a reaction against Bill Clinton; they saw Newt as some mean, power-hungry guy who happened to catch a wave at the right time. But I found a 1979 *USA Today* article in which the then-freshman congressman from Georgia had predicted he would take over the House by the end of the 1980s. His brash prediction was off by just a few years; in other words, Newt had been planning and working for this moment for nearly fifteen years. Early on, he had taken over a moribund GOP outfit called GOPAC and turned it into a candidate-recruiting and educational powerhouse.

More important, it became obvious to me that Newt was a world-class intellectual, who was basing his movement on a consistent, rigorous view of American history. With the Cold War over and new economic challenges arising, serious people were looking for serious answers about America's future—and Newt had them. He had a theory about the country's legacy and its destiny that gave coherence to everything he did and said. In his mind, the United States had been founded by exceptional, heroic men who had developed the best possible system of government to preserve liberty. But in the twentieth century, from the New Deal through the Great Society, the liberals had ruined it. He was on a crusade to return the republic to its philosophical roots and restore American liberty. Everything he did was tied back to that simple, galvanizing, and transformative mission. In some ways, it was standard conservative fare. But Newt borrowed from a wide range of leading-edge thinkers—from Peter Drucker to Alvin Toffler—to make his ideas sing.

No prominent Democrat on the scene at the time had anything like it. Not even close.

I believed—then and now—in the power of stories and ideas.
Newt's narratives and concepts had won the day. While many liberal commentators were content to call him names, I wanted to
understand his strategy and the appeal of his message. Even
though I was just a young civil-rights attorney in the San Francisco Bay Area, I thought it was important to challenge myself.
How would I stand up to such an impressive suite of arguments?
How could liberals fight back at the same level of depth, with the
same tactical and rhetorical skill? So I spent a decade or more
debating Newt Gingrich in my mind—trying to generate re-
sponses that could go toe-to-toe with his narrative. For years, I
continued to buy every book, watch every speech, read every opinion piece I could get my hands on. My engagement with his ideas
had a dual impact on me. On the one hand, I found his patriotism
infectious. His pride in the founders' achievement rubbed off on
me in ways that surprised me. As a result, I found myself growing
frustrated with some liberals' reluctance to champion and celebrate the great things about our country. After all, it is hard to lead
a nation you don't love.

At the same time, I began to zero in on a key difference between Newt's brand of patriotism and my own. In Newt's narrative, it sometimes seemed that the American republic was born
nearly perfect but then fell from grace. But in my mind, our nation
was born imperfect, and it has been climbing ever since. In trying
to make sense of this dissonance, I came to realize that America
is two things—not one. Our nation's founding reality was ugly and
unequal—with few rights for women, nonwhites, and property-
less white men. But our nation's founding dream is beautiful,
rooted in the conviction that all are created equal. Progressive
patriots don't want to restore anything; we want to progress away
from the ugliness of the founding reality and toward the beauty of

the founding dream. (I will share more on these ideas in the conclusion of the book.)

My point here is that my intellectual wrangling with Newt's ideas forced me to deepen and clarify my relationship to America's story. I arrived at a synthesis that let me love my country and challenge it, too. I had never met Newt in person, but he had been the ideal intellectual adversary to help me develop my own philosophy.

And then, years later, I found myself face-to-face with the man himself.

It was late summer 2013. I was at the Washington, D.C., office of CNN to meet with the network's top brass and discuss the possibility of doing a show there. The idea was to bring back *Crossfire*, a classic program that had once defined CNN. Newt and I would be two of the co-hosts—along with Obama White House alum Stephanie Cutter and rising conservative media darling S. E. Cupp (who has since become one of my closest friends).

I entered a medium-sized conference room, and there he was—Newt Gingrich himself, surrounded by aides. He wore an ensemble I recognized from watching countless TV interviews: a dark blazer, a white shirt, and a red tie. Seeing him in the flesh was surreal.

I was as prepared as I'd ever be for this important introduction, so I walked right up to him. He stood up, and I shook his hand. "I want you to know," I said, mid-handshake, "I'm the only person in the United States, including your wife"—I hesitated, letting him wonder where I was going with this—"who's read all your books, sir." He looked pleasantly surprised. He knew who I was, and I'm pretty sure that's not what he thought he'd hear out of my mouth as a greeting.

"Really?" His surprise was genuine. Everything about me, from my background to my history as an activist to my progressive politics, perhaps made me the least likely reader of Newt's impressive booklist.

"Yes, I've read all of them," I confirmed. "In hardback!"

Defying all reasonable expectations, Newt Gingrich and I hit it off. He was even more brilliant one-on-one than his public persona suggested. He worked to make the whole production team better, often through deceptively simple suggestions related to language. Reviewing our written instructions on the flow of the show, Newt suggested to our producers: "Rather than 'question the guests,' perhaps we should 'engage the guests.'" This one recommendation profoundly and permanently impacted the tenor of our show. Newt even took time to give me pointers about how to handle myself on television or sharpen my arguments. A true master of debate understands all sides of an issue, and he wanted everyone on the show to do their best—even the Democrats with whom he was dueling. Watching him close up, I could see how he was able to take his ragtag conservative minority in the House and transform it into a winning, dominant electoral force.

As we worked on the show together, Newt and I discovered that we had an unlikely unifying passion: reforming the criminal-justice system. He told me that many conservatives were disgusted by what was going on in U.S. prisons. In his mind, the prison system had become a giant failing government bureaucracy. Libertarians in his party were concerned about the government gobbling up too many rights and encroaching on individual freedoms. Christian conservatives lamented the fact that formerly incarcerated people were given almost no chance for redemption—violating a key value for Christians. It is true: Even after someone serves her sentence and repays her debt to society, she leaves a physical prison and enters a social prison—in which she often is not allowed to vote, rent an apartment, or get a student loan.

I was moved and inspired to hear such a powerful right-wing critique of an issue usually associated with bleeding-heart liberals. When I told him that I wished he would bring his prison concerns up more publicly, Newt said that he had spoken publicly on the issue many times. He credited a group called Right on Crime for his conversion on the issues. He pointed out that many conservatives were taking action. In fact, Republican governors already had passed more legislation to address the crisis than their Democratic counterparts. He praised Ohio's governor, John Kasich, and Texas's governor, Rick Perry. Perry had closed three prisons in Texas as a part of a program that brought down the prison budget as well as the crime rate. Georgia governor Nathan Deal was also way out front.

Republicans were leading the charge on prison reform, but liberals hadn't noticed—or wouldn't recognize—their work. As a dedicated advocate for prison reform, this hole in my own knowledge embarrassed me. I vowed to be better informed. I also saw the opportunity for real progress in fixing our broken criminal-justice system through genuine unity between the left and the right.

Both Newt and I wondered if we could put our shared philosophical ground into practice. He mused, "If we could get one hundred people, on a truly bipartisan basis, to come together in Washington, D.C., for just one hour, we could probably turn criminal-justice reform into a bipartisan issue."

So I asked my colleague Jessica Jackson to pull together a hundred politicians from both sides of the party line. She failed: We got eight hundred, not one hundred—and they stayed for eight hours, not one hour. (You will hear more about Jessica, the Dream Corps, and the fight for criminal-justice reform later in this book.) Suffice it to say that more than a dozen Congress members participated in our summit, as did three GOP governors and three Obama cabinet secretaries. Obama himself sent a video. As a direct result of our "Bipartisan Summit on Criminal Justice Reform," three bills to reform the criminal-justice system were introduced in Congress. None has yet become law, but the idea that criminal-justice reform was one place where Democrats and Republicans could work together quickly became conventional wisdom. Our summit played an important role in that process. Newt was right.

The former Speaker once told me something profound, as we discussed ways to think about bipartisanship: "Your 'ninety percent enemy' can still be your 'ten percent friend'—on every point where you agree." Newt and I still passionately disagree on 90 percent or more of the issues. But in those places where our views align, we look for ways to work together. When it comes to topics like fixing the justice system or ending the opioid epidemic, we owe it to ordinary people to try.

IT IS STRANGE WHEN YOUR philosophical enemy becomes your political friend. It is perhaps even stranger when your musical hero becomes your personal champion. But it happened to me—at a time when I really needed some help.

My hero wore a purple cape. And he showed me how much good is possible when people with public platforms care less about getting credit and more about uplifting communities.

Back in the mid-2000s, on a day like any other, I was sitting in my Oakland office when I opened an envelope to find a large check for an anonymous donation for my "Green For All" initiative in California. This was a project that taught young people about careers in sustainable energy, what I call "green-collar" jobs. We wanted to leverage the momentum around clean-energy industries and pass on real opportunities to the youth in our community. Opportunities included training people to install solar panels, weatherize buildings, put up green roofs. I figured that the work we were doing must've caught this anonymous donor's attention because I'd been on the news recently, talking about creating the first ever Green Jobs Corps with the support of the Oakland City Council.

I had a practice of never accepting anonymous gifts—you had to know exactly where the money was coming from. Running a social-justice nonprofit, I didn't ever want to use funds from unsavory sources. I sent that check back to the return address immediately.

A few weeks later, the check came back. I returned it again. That back-and-forth happened a third time before someone who identified himself as a lawyer called me up to ask me to cash it already. I told him my policy on anonymous gifts, and he got nervous, as if not getting me to cash the check would get him in trouble. The lawyer begged me to accept the donation, but I held my ground. Finally, sounding desperate, he said, "I can't tell you who it is, but I can tell you his favorite color is purple."

I was floored. Prince? *The* Prince? I was a lifelong fan, going back to his very first album. "Well, now you have another problem," I said to his lawyer. "I can't cash the check, because I'm going to frame it!"

I guess the lawyer told Prince what I'd said, and he thought that was pretty funny, because soon thereafter Prince got in touch with me himself. Through back-and-forths on the phone and through intermediaries, we started building a friendship. Out of that, we eventually worked on many positive transformative projects together.

It turns out that Prince wasn't doing anything unusual when he sent me that terrifically helpful check. Prince did this all the time.

For example, on a sunny afternoon in New York City, the Harlem Children's Zone founder, Geoffrey Canada, received his own shocking phone call. "Prince would like to speak with you," the voice on the other end of the line said. Despite the directness of the sentence, Geoffrey couldn't make sense of the information. Prince Charles had recently visited the Harlem Children's Zone— why was he calling?

"Prince Charles?" he tried to clarify.

"No," the caller responded. "Prince—*the* Prince."

Geoffrey couldn't believe it, either. He heard a few muffled shufflings and then another voice came to the phone, a much more familiar one. The rock star told Geoffrey, "I want to help you. I don't want anybody else to know about this. I just want to help you. I want to give the Harlem Children's Zone a million dollars out of my tour."

Geoffrey almost fell out of his seat. "Did you just say you're going to give us a million dollars?"

Prince confirmed it. Yes, he did; yes, he was.

"But we can't tell anybody about it?" Geoffrey asked.

"It'll ruin it if anybody hears," Prince said. "When you've been blessed the way I have, you have to give back. You don't do it in a way that makes people say what a wonderful person you are. You just do it." Soon thereafter, the Harlem Children's Zone received an "anonymous" donation of one million dollars.

The organizing guru Alicia Garza, co-creator of the Black Lives Matter Network, also received a generous donation. In fact, Prince gave some of the very first donations to Black Lives Matter. For the movement, Prince's money certainly helped. But, as Alicia noted, "It was really important in its symbolism, important in its very clear statement that he believed in what we were doing and that what we were doing was important." Later, when Prince strolled out in shimmering orange, twirling his cane, to announce Best Album at the 2015 Grammys, he made sure to highlight his support (though not his monetary contributions) of BLM to the millions of viewers watching: "Albums still matter. Like books, and black lives, albums still matter. Tonight, and always."

Prince made more anonymous donations than I know. It's a number known only to him and God. But from talking to him over the years, I would say that 85 to 95 percent of the other people he helped had no idea he aided them. No idea. Whether these folks were part of a youth program or art program or were in legal trouble, they would have no idea who paid their bill. That's how he operated.

When I resigned in 2009 from the White House as special adviser on green jobs, I left under a firestorm of criticism. President Obama's Republican opponents sensationalized past statements I'd made and distorted my history of grassroots activism in order to build a personal smear campaign—the worst kind of partisan politics.* At first I was inundated with calls, from across the political spectrum, to stay and fight. But I didn't want to fight for myself; I took on the appointment with President Obama because I wanted to fight for others and for the future of our environment and our young people. I didn't want my presence to tarnish Obama's first year in office with controversy. I knew it was time for me to go.

When you're in the White House, people rush toward you. After I left the White House, the phone stopped ringing. No one called anymore. I was in a very low place.

One of the people who called me during that time? Prince. He invited me to visit his home in Minneapolis. A black SUV picked me up from the airport and we drove to Prince's compound, the legendary Paisley Park, where he lived and recorded music.

I couldn't believe I was actually stepping foot inside Prince's home! I used to sketch pictures of him when I was a kid; I even gave one as a present to a girl whom I liked. I was beyond star-

---

* I had never even hoped for a job in the Obama White House, but in March 2009 I was honored to accept an appointment as Special Adviser for Green Jobs, Enterprise, and Innovation at the White House Council on Environmental Quality. The work was challenging and important; I ran the interagency process that oversaw more than 80 billion dollars in green projects and clean-energy investments, as a part of the 2009 stimulus package. Unfortunately, that summer some right-wing critics in the media started attacking me over my left-wing activist past. Most vociferous was Fox News's Glenn Beck. Beck had a special motive: He was reeling from an advertiser boycott spearheaded by an organization I had co-founded, ColorOfChange.org. Led by Beck, my critics made hay over the fact that I had once belonged to a socialist collective and called for a new trial for Mumia Abu-Jamal, a black journalist who may have been wrongfully convicted of killing a police officer. But they wrongly claimed that I had signed a 2004 911Truth.org petition—a document that questioned whether President George W. Bush had "allowed" 9/11 to happen in some way. About a year later, 911Truth.org was forced to acknowledge that I had not signed their petition, but in 2009 the smear campaign was under way and I felt I was becoming a distraction from the goals of the Obama administration. I resigned in early September 2009.

struck. When you enter Paisley Park, there's a long corridor lined with Grammys, American Music Awards, MTV Awards—an astounding testimony to Prince's singular achievements as an artist. His iconic purple motorcycle, the one he rode in the movie *Purple Rain,* is right there in the foyer! I must have looked crazy, walking along with my hands pressed to my sides, not wanting to mess anything up. It was unreal, a truly magical place that reflected Prince's artistry and extraordinary mind.

Excited as I was, I also felt a great sense of calm at Paisley Park, a kind of joy and peace that I had never before experienced. This building—and everything in it—was the brainchild of one man, a rebel who had decided to live life on his own terms. Prince Rogers Nelson had grown up poor and black in a white, affluent town in Minnesota. More important: That city—indeed, the entire Twin Cities area of Minneapolis and St. Paul—was itself a marginal backwater compared to more famous entertainment capitals like New York City or Los Angeles. In other words: Prince was born on the margins of the margin. And yet he had propelled himself to the very center of global pop culture. This massive complex—the fabled Paisley Park—was a monument to what genius, unleashed, could accomplish. Being there, I felt reaffirmed in my belief—instilled in me by my parents—that hard work and perseverance could overcome any obstacle. Looking around at all Prince had achieved, I felt proud of him and all the underdogs everywhere who beat the odds and make their marks.

I waited in a small reception area for the megastar to arrive. The minutes stretched to nearly an hour. Then, from somewhere in the dark recesses of the building, I heard the distinctive clicking of high heels. I strained to determine which direction the sound was coming from. But the complex is built like a series of hangar-sized warehouses, residences, and performance spaces, so I couldn't tell for sure. The steps got closer; the clicks got louder.

Then suddenly Prince himself was right in front of me—a diminutive figure wearing a brightly colored shirt and shoes that lit up with each step. "Welcome," he said, in that distinctive baritone. "Are you hungry? We can eat upstairs." He strolled right past me toward an elevator. He was acting as if I were a regular guest, so I just went along with it. We made our way upstairs to a conference room, passing a cage on the way that held two white doves. I thought about the first time I had heard his hit song "When Doves Cry," when I was in high school. I never thought I would ever be in Prince's home, seeing his doves with my own eyes.

Prince and I sat in the conference room and talked for nearly six hours, about everything from religion to the inner functions of the federal government. At one point, he just stopped and looked at me. "You seem really sad."

He was right. I'd been out of the White House for only a few weeks, and I was still feeling all the pain and sorrow. "I lost a great job," I said to him.

"You're still sad about that?" Prince said. "I wouldn't worry too much about it."

How could I not worry? At that point, I thought my career was over. Everything I had worked so hard for had been washed away by a few days of false accusations, distortions, and scandalous headlines. I had no idea what I was going to do next with my life.

"I wouldn't worry about it," he said again. "Way worse things than that are going to happen to you."

That comment stunned me. But Prince said it with such a calm assurance that it actually made me feel better somehow.

I leaned forward in my chair and asked, "Why do you say that?"

He looked at me for a long time. Then he said, "Look, you're one of those people who is really committed to justice, right?" I nodded. "Well, stuff like that happens to guys like you all the time."

If anyone else had said those same words, they would have

sounded like a curse, but from Prince, I welcomed them. He had elevated me into that rare club of people who pay a price for trying to make a difference. He respected me more, not less, for having endured the slings and arrows of public life. In fact, Prince saw my scars as badges of honor. My own pain and shame had not let me see things that way before. For the first time, I could imagine coming to terms with my loss, picking myself up, and moving forward.

Seeing that his comments had landed well, Prince gave me some advice. "Go to Jerusalem. Just pray there for a couple weeks," he said. "When you come back, take a blank piece of paper and write down everything that you think needs to happen. Everything that will advance the cause. Write it down, just as if you were still working in the White House."

"Okay," I said. "I will."

"Good," he said. "Then bring that list to me. And I'll help you get it done."

That pledge of royal assistance became my North Star; I turned my face to it whenever my sadness and depression blocked out the sun. I did go to Jerusalem and make that list. But after such a hard public fall, it took me more than a year to get my feet under me again emotionally. During that time, I consumed a ton of self-help books, got some counseling, attended a Pema Chödrön meditation retreat, and even spent ten days healing and reflecting at the Hoffman Institute. When I felt ready to climb back onto the public stage, I went back to Prince, and we got to work. When I next mounted the public stage, I did so with a deeper sense of inner security. I had healed some hurts that ran much deeper than just the pain of leaving a good job in D.C. In addition to that, having a megastar in your corner gives you a huge amount of extra confidence. Even if you are just a minor hero, like Robin, you walk with more swagger when you know that you can always call on a major superhero like Batman in a pinch. Prince was my Batman.

In 2012, we put on a series of concerts in Chicago to promote community healing and voter registration. The concerts gave visibility to my newest initiative: Rebuild the Dream, a precursor to the Dream Corps, which I help run today. The actress Rosario Dawson helped out. Entertainers like Jennifer Hudson and Janelle Monae made guest appearances at the shows. In a rare media appearance to promote the initiative, Prince discussed it on *The View*, along with Rosario and me. When *The View* co-host Sherri Shepherd asked Prince why he was joining forces with Rosario and me, he spoke quietly and with great conviction and urgency.

"We're at a place now in this country where we're going to have to work together and stop looking at each other's affiliation and start taking care of each other. It's desperate times."

Prince was never motivated by any desire for public credit. He just wanted to help those who were less fortunate. He recognized the challenges ahead, and in his own selfless way, he challenged all of us to meet them.

In 2014, Prince and I launched #YesWeCode at the Essence Festival with a concert for fifty thousand people. At the festival, we also sponsored a youth-focused hackathon to teach young people coding skills. That initiative came straight out of Prince's imagination: What if kids in the hood could upload apps instead of just downloading them? A remarkable young lady named Victoria Pannell won the #YesWeCode hackathon competition that year. She'd never done app development before she showed up for the festival! You know what she told me? That learning how to code that day made her feel truly empowered for the first time. She said, "Young people often feel like we don't have a voice. We're told not to speak up." After winning the hackathon, Victoria said, she felt freedom, like she could go on to do anything.

I'm willing to bet that there are thousands of stories like this out there. Prince touched people's lives in countless ways. Working with him on these humanitarian projects changed me. Prince wanted to make sure people's gifts and talents had a chance to shine. He hated the idea that you couldn't blossom just because of your skin color, your gender, or where you were born. Initiatives like #YesWeCode gave kids the ability to code what they wanted to code and be empowered because of it.

His music will be his legacy, always and forever, but I will always remember him for his generous commitment to giving back. As much as Prince was a musical genius, the same guy was there behind the scenes, brainstorming solutions, sending help to people who most needed it. He didn't want the public to know, because he didn't want credit. But I feel it's important to talk about now. It's a part of his legacy I want people to remember.

Working so closely with Prince came with certain perks, of course. I got to see him perform in concert, up close and personal, and I learned something profound at his shows. Prince would often seat his friends on sofas in the wings of the stage when he performed. This is an extraordinary place from which to watch any concert, let alone a concert by one of the great master showmen of all time. Usually, when you're in the audience at a concert, you can see only the artist onstage, the backs of people's heads, and maybe a few cellphones hoisted high to record the event. Sitting onstage as Prince's guest, I witnessed a very different scene. I got to see him and the band, of course, but I also got to look out into the faces of all the people as they stared up to watch the show.

On many nights I glimpsed every color and kind of human being, with their eyes wide, their mouths half open and smiling, brought together by one man's musical genius. Prince's music created an environment where everyone fit in somehow. The punk rockers and the nerds, the R&B fanatics and the rappers. White, brown, black, young, and old. Nobody was a guest or a voyeur at a Prince concert. Somehow everyone was in on the secret of the purple magic that he created, and everyone belonged. One reason that I believe that people can come together across every conceivable line of division—what I keep talking about throughout this book—is that I've seen it with my own eyes.

I've witnessed humanity united, even momentarily, by one man striking a single note on his guitar. I believe that everybody has a note inside that they can strike, which can resonate beyond their own skin color or political ideology. They may do it through community service. They may do it through their profession. They may do it through parenting. But everyone has that something, that spark, and we have a responsibility to offer it to the world.

There is a painful irony in devoting a section of this book to Prince's anonymous philanthropy. He never wanted to stamp his name on any project. But I think revealing his name now multiplies the power of his approach to giving—by encouraging others to follow his example of generous and selfless support for those most in need.

When I emerged from the shower early in the morning on April 21, 2016, and picked up the phone, I was completely shaken by the news of Prince's passing. I had no idea Prince was addicted to prescription pain medication or that he was suffering so much. Like many others who've lost a loved one to addiction, I've spent hours racking my brain, thinking of what I could have done differently, or better. My quest for answers brought me face-to-face with the depth and scope of this national epidemic, and I've committed myself to finding a way to end opioid abuse as a result.

Prince's presence in my life was a miracle, for which I still have no explanation, and his exit was a devastating tragedy, for which I still have no words. We lost him too soon. But I keep marching on with the beautiful work we started. He rarely saw humanity in terms of red or blue. When he saw people with problems, the solutions were always purple.

The rest of us could learn a lot from him.

CHAPTER SIX

THE BEAUTIFUL WORK: FOUR SOLUTIONS

I MAGINE THIS. AT A LARGE FAMILY REUNION, SOMEONE'S BE-loved toddler wanders off from the picnic area and falls down a well. Everyone rushes over and—terrified—peers down the dark shaft. The little girl is down there. She's hurt and crying, but she's alive.

Though crazed with worry, a number of relatives start to point fingers. The Republicans in the family blame the Democrats for being too lenient and not teaching the child to obey instructions. The Democrats in their ranks in turn blame the Republican family members for being too stingy and not helping to pay for the childcare the parents have needed.

The argument rages back and forth, at a higher and higher pitch. Finally, the child's desperate parents just ask, *"Please*—can you all *please* just help us get our baby out of the well?"

It turns out one of the Republicans has a strong truck but no rope to lower down the well. A Democrat has a long garden hose in the back of his car, but his fuel-efficient hybrid isn't designed for pulling.

So the feud starts back up again. Why would *anyone* buy a

sissy car like that? Why would *you* buy a truck that pollutes the earth? Why is *your* trunk full of crappy groceries from corporations? Why do *you* think that growing hippie food makes you better than everyone?

As the insults fly back and forth, the parents throw up their hands and decide to take action on their own. They attach the Democrat's hose to the back of the Republican's truck, lower the improvised lifeline down into the pit, and manage to lift the baby to freedom.

In an emergency, our worst family members always turn on each other. But our best family members always turn to each other. They put aside their differences, come together, and focus on solving the problem at hand. Half the time, it turns out that the differences within the family emerge as sources of strength.

I think you likely know where I'm going with this: Today, our nation faces a series of national emergencies—any one of which should bring us all together. But our national leaders seem to be standing around every well, screaming at each other. It's like a giant food fight. Republicans throw meat, and the Democrats throw vegetables. Each attack becomes another occasion to rally one's side—and heave another volley at the opposition. Both sides yell out their slogans and generate mayhem. And, honestly, I don't think they are going to stop anytime soon.

In the meantime, no matter which side of the family you identify with, each individual American must decide: Do you want to be one of the bickering in-laws? Or do you want to be one of the parents?

Here, I write for the parents and want to call your attention to some of the pressing emergencies to which we might turn our collective attention. Each involves areas where conservatives and progressives have complementary values and skill sets. My hope is that by finding a few areas of common purpose, we can bring out the best in both sides. And maybe begin to come together, in a new way.

*

MATTERS OF LIFE AND DEATH tend to bring out our best—like when a baby falls down a well. Perhaps we should start our search for unity where Americans are actually dying. Where are the death rates unacceptably high? Where are American families gathering in graveyards, too soon and too often?

The data is clear. Americans are dying in Appalachia. They are dying in Chicago. Dying at the U.S.–Mexico border. Dying on Native American reservations. Dying in Flint, Michigan. There are hundreds of similar centers of pain in our country, some less famous than others.

What's the common denominator with the high death rates? Sometimes it's poverty. Sometimes it's addiction. Often it's a broken criminal-justice system. Those scourges are as present in West Virginia as they are in South Central Los Angeles. The races of the community members may differ; they may speak English with different accents, or no English at all. But they share the same pain.

In a healthy society, common pain should lead to common purpose. Common purpose should lead to common projects. And common projects should bring back common sense.

For those of us who want to act like parents in this situation, I propose some common projects we can work on together.

FIX THE JUSTICE SYSTEM

The last place in America you would expect to find common ground is a prison cell. But with our prison population ballooning, liberals and conservatives are finding common cause in fixing the criminal-justice system.

The reason is simple—and shameful: The United States, a beacon of liberty for so many, is now the number one incarcerator of human beings in the world. We jail more of our own citizens than China, which is several times larger in population. We have only 5 percent of the world's population but a whopping 25 percent of the world's prisoners. That means one out of every four humans locked up anywhere on earth is imprisoned here, in the "land of the free." Whether you care about protecting individual liberty from an intrusive government or are committed to social justice for all, you should be greatly alarmed by our broken criminal-justice system. Consider this:

Right now, instead of taking care of their families or contributing to their communities or our economy, nearly one in every hundred Americans is behind bars. In forty years, the total number of people in prison or jail in America has grown by nearly 500 percent, far outpacing population growth. The federal-prison population has grown 800 percent in thirty years, with nearly half of the people there for drug-related offenses.

We have created a ravenous system that must be fed—at a cost of 80 billion taxpayer dollars a year in prison expenditures alone. In California, it costs more to house a prisoner for a year than it does to cover the entire cost—tuition, books, room, board, and a sweet social life—of a year at Harvard University. When factoring in lost economic productivity and social costs, the total cost reaches upward of one trillion dollars per year. One American child out of every twenty-eight—that's 2.8 million American children—has a parent in jail or prison. Approximately five million children will have experienced parental incarceration at some point in their lives.

The nightmare doesn't end after people have served their time. More than 70 million Americans have a criminal record, which essentially prohibits them from accessing basic employment, housing, or financial support for continued education or job-skill development. In many states, voter laws prohibit people with felony convictions from participating in our democracy. An estimated 6.1 million Americans who live in our communities and work in our economy are denied the right to vote solely based on a past felony conviction. Americans who care about redemption and second chances have a reason to be heartbroken.

Whatever your political persuasion, these numbers should not numb you. They should motivate you. One of the few things that a growing number of liberals and conservatives agree upon today is this: The United States locks up too many people, for too long, at too high a cost, often for unjustifiable reasons and with indefensible results. Our broken criminal-justice system is a fundamental threat to our safety, our security, and our democracy. The entire system is deep down in the well, and it is up to us to pull it out.

The good news? We can.

When ordinary Americans take action on the issues that most affect their lives, inspiring change is possible. Take Jessica Jackson, for example.

Jessica and her first husband were a young, middle-class white couple living in Georgia. They owned a home, and Jessica was pregnant with their first child, a daughter. Like a growing number of white rural Americans, her husband struggled with addiction. Shortly after their daughter was born, her husband was arrested. At first, Jessica was almost relieved—she hoped that he would get the help he so desperately needed to overcome his addiction. Instead, he was slapped with a sentence of fifteen years in prison.

Jessica was blindsided by the sentence, but she wasn't about to watch her life go down the drain. The gross injustice facing her family lit a fire in her. Despite the circumstances, she fought tooth and nail, while working and raising her daughter, to earn her college degree and eventually a law degree. When I met her at a 2012 Marin County campaign event to reelect Obama, she was a human-rights attorney representing death-penalty clients in California. Her first words to me were a direct personal challenge: "What are you doing to help the people locked in cages?"

My focus was green jobs at that point, but I still had some good war stories. I told her of my years of criminal-justice work in Oakland—my efforts to disrupt the "school to jail" pipeline by founding the Ella Baker Center For Human Rights shortly after law school; my unsuccessful fight to defeat a California ballot measure called Prop 21, which put sixteen-year-olds in adult prisons; my prolonged and successful battle to stop Oakland's "super jail" for youth. She was unimpressed.

"That was ten years ago," she said. "What are you doing now?"

Like so many young activists who threw their hearts and souls into the fight against the prison system, working to fix the criminal-justice system had taken a personal toll on me. It's heartbreaking, exhausting work, with a human face for every tragedy or setback. I have nothing but respect for those who devote their lives to it. I had dedicated nearly fifteen years of my life to the work before I finally—I thought—limped away for good. And yet here was this young woman on a personal crusade. I could not refuse her request for help, if only to pass along some key lessons. Since I first met her, and through the force of her genius and will, Jessica has built her personal mission into a national movement for bipartisan justice reform.

Jessica's focus and dedication in the face of her family's ordeal pulled me back into the fight to reform the justice system. Early in her career, Jessica was also frustrated and exhausted. Death-row legal work is brutal. You hope a judge or a clerk will read your pages of legal work and fact-finding before your client is killed, but most cases end in defeat of the most lasting kind. Instead of giving up, Jessica recognized that death-row issues were only a symptom of a much greater problem. So she took on the entire beast.

Eventually, Jessica introduced me to a young Stanford Law School grad named Matt Haney. Matt had recently been elected to the San Francisco school board and was interested in tackling the school-to-prison pipeline. Matt is super smart, personable, and charismatic. A veteran of the 2008 Obama campaign, he seems to know everyone, everywhere, and is beloved by all. Yet beneath his easy charm is a steadfast, relentless fighter against racism.

He learned early the weight of his white privilege, when he and a close friend named Kevin were arrested at a house party the evening before Matt was set to leave for college. Matt was treated fairly and with respect by the police officers, while the police did everything in their power to pin the incident on Kevin, who was African American. As a juvenile, Kevin had spent time in jail, where he was scarred and victimized by being locked up with men nearly twice his age. Not long after the house-party incident, Kevin tragically took his own life.

Each of us had had our own heartbreaking exposure to the criminal-injustice system. Together, Jessica, Matt, and I saw unprecedented opportunity to roll back mass incarceration. So we founded #cut50 in July 2014, as a national initiative to cut by 50 percent the crime rate and the U.S. prison population.

It's important to remember the state of politics in 2014. The Tea Party was still a major force. Whatever Obama proposed, the Tea Party–backed Republicans blocked; whatever the Tea Party tried to pass, Obama vetoed. This tribal gridlock in D.C. consumed large chunks of people's time. To get anything done, progressives needed to figure out a way to work with Republicans on common-ground issues.

And what miracle strategist and passionate Republican politician did I know who could help us get the job done? Newt Gingrich, or course. At first, Jessica was hesitant. After all, she had lived in Georgia—Newt's home state—and she thought he was an unlikely bedfellow indeed. But she understood the potential of our collaboration.

When Newt suggested we pull together a bipartisan summit,

Jessica worked tirelessly to build support around the idea. It was Jessica who raised our goal from one hundred people for one hour to eight hundred for a whole day. She and Matt were whizzing proposals and invitations in every direction. Oh yeah, and Jessica had just given birth to her second child. In fact, on the day of one of the press events leading up to the summit, she had gone into labor. She was still making calls, shooting off directions, and advising on final decisions from the hospital! She didn't even tell anyone where she was.

Before March 2015, the idea of "bipartisan criminal-justice reform" was an oxymoron. Soon afterward, the idea would become so widely accepted as to become cliché.

Among the eight hundred summit attendees were eighty-four featured speakers, including Eric Holder, then–attorney general, plus Newt Gingrich in a conversation with Senator Cory Booker of New Jersey. Nathan Deal, the Republican governor of Georgia, was our luncheon keynote speaker. President Barack Obama sent us a video featuring an intimate sit-down with David Simon, the creator of the HBO series *The Wire,* tacitly endorsing our efforts. The conservative former California assemblyman Pat Nolan, who served prison time himself, was a speaker; so was the legendary Democratic Party strategist Donna Brazile. We had more than a dozen sponsors from both the left and the right, including the ACLU and Koch Industries. One of the speakers, #cut50's own Shaka Senghor, had served nineteen years in prison for second-degree homicide and spoke from that crushing experience. (A happy update: Shaka went on to publish the *New York Times*–bestselling memoir *Writing My Wrongs.*) If you closed your eyes, you couldn't tell, listening to people talk, which speakers were the Republicans and which ones were the Democrats.

Three bipartisan federal bills were announced at the summit: The Comprehensive Justice and Mental Health Act, the reauthorization of the Juvenile Justice and Delinquency Prevention Act, and the Police CAMERA Act. Several more were announced shortly thereafter. One of those bills, the Comprehensive Justice and Mental Health Act—which was led by an unlikely cast of Republicans and Democrats, including Senator Al Franken of Minnesota and Congressman Doug Collins of Georgia—would be signed into law by President Barack Obama. The bill became an integral portion of a last-minute package of bills to address mental-health and opioid-addiction treatment in the waning days of his administration. We helped make it completely safe and possible to collaborate on a tough issue—in a town where two sides are hunkered down with a "no-man's-land" in the middle. We decided to walk out into that middle ground and plant a flag in the soil—not to start a war, but to end one. Lots of people marched with us. And the work continues.

By the way, Jessica is now the mayor of Mill Valley, California, on top of overseeing #cut50. Of course.

As Jessica's personal story suggests, no one in our country—black, brown, or white, rural or urban—is immune to the viral threat our broken justice system presents. The astronomical rates of incarceration and the billions of dollars we pour into prisons affect us all. There is no question that race is a factor in this broken system. Many prisons that I've visited look like slave ships on dry land. Black men make up about 6.5 percent of the U.S. population but 40.2 percent of the prison population. They're imprisoned at much higher rates than white men, even if they commit similar crimes. Latino men and black women also face disproportionately high imprisonment rates. Unconstitutional programs like "stop and frisk" criminalize black and brown youth and wreak havoc on communities. African Americans and whites do illegal drugs at roughly the same rates, and yet African Americans are incarcerated at six times the rates of whites for identical drug-related offenses.

But mass incarceration isn't just a race issue. *The New York*

Times reported on Dearborn County, Indiana, a county that proudly sends to jail more people per capita than any other county in the United States. One in every ten adults is either in prison, jail, or on probation. The kicker? Dearborn County is 97 percent white. While black and brown communities have borne the brunt of our exploding incarceration industry, it's now impacting white rural communities worse than ever before.

As a result, leaders of all colors, classes, and creeds have renewed personal incentives to take a much harder look at America's prison problem. But making much-needed progress on our broken justice system is not a slam dunk, by any means. Trump's attorney general, Jeff Sessions, seems to be hell-bent on reinvigorating the war on drugs with harsh sentencing and prosecutorial charging policies that are out of step with both the data and his own party on this issue. Others are leading in a smarter direction. U.S. senator Rand Paul (Republican of Kentucky) has introduced or co-sponsored more than twenty-five bills on criminal justice. Tea Party favorite U.S. senator Mike Lee (Republican of Utah) sponsored the Smarter Sentencing Act, to curtail draconian sentencing. "I support this bill not in spite of the fact that I want public safety but because of it," Lee said. "Separating a potentially productive person from his or her family and support network, and branding him a felon for life, less likely to find or keep a job, is counterproductive to society's interests." Instead of building prisons, Texas governor Rick Perry oversaw a transformation of Texas's criminal-justice system by shifting funds into alternatives like drug courts, treatment programs, and jobs. From 2007 to 2015, the rate of incarceration in Texas dropped by 14 percent; crime rates fell by 29 percent, beating the national average. The state closed three prisons. He left Texas with its lowest crime rate since 1968, and recidivism is 7 percent less than it was before the 2007 reform effort. Perry's work became the model for conservative-led justice-reform efforts, championed by powerful and well-respected organizations like Right on Crime, FreedomWorks, and the American Conservative Union Foundation, which have spurred dozens of other governors and state legislatures to take action.

To those on the left who may cringe at my celebration of these conservative prison reformers, I will repeat what Jessica told the audience at the bipartisan summit: "When it was my husband who was incarcerated, I didn't care if it was a law introduced by a Republican or by a Democrat that brought him home. I just wanted him to come home." The people who are most impacted don't much care about partisan infighting. They want and need change. The strongest lock keeping them imprisoned is gridlock. Only bipartisan solutions can set them free.

Let's implement some.

Here is a list of ten things that both conservatives and liberals agree will help fix our prison system and minimize its devastating impact on communities. Conservative leaders have incorporated these ideas into laws and actions in their cities and states. You can find more details of individual efforts and groups from both the left and the right leading the fight in the appendixes.

1. Dismantle the School-to-Prison Pipeline

For too many young people, schools aren't just places for learning or education—they are a primer for involvement in the justice system. As with our prisons and jails, it's students of color who are disproportionately impacted by failing schools, overly harsh discipline policies, and police roaming the hallways. The solution is simple and has already been implemented. In San Francisco, school-board member and #cut50 co-founder Matt Haney introduced sweeping reforms to the district's discipline and suspension policies. The "Safe and Supportive Schools" policy is based on the concept that it's better to keep kids in school rather than suspend or expel them for minor infractions. The result: a dramatic reduction in suspensions, expulsions, and arrests, especially for students of color.

2. Eliminate Overuse of Fees and Fines

Underfunded courts and police departments across the country are on the hunt for new revenue. Their solution has been to target the poorest and most vulnerable with a bevy of fees and fines associated with almost every point of interaction in the criminal-justice system—going so far as to even charge juveniles for the time they spend in detention. The problem has gotten so bad that about ten million people owe a total of 50 billion dollars in debt to court and prison systems across the country. To fix this, we should fund our criminal-justice system through ordinary budgetary processes rather than relying on cash-register justice on the backs of the poorest and most vulnerable. Courts should also start considering whether individuals can actually pay the fee or fine that's being imposed and, if not, offer alternatives like community service, which contributes to the public good rather than leaving people debt-burdened indefinitely. When organizations on polar opposites of the political spectrum—from ALEC to the ACLU—agree, there's no excuse for not fixing this.

3. Abolish Money Bail

Often, freedom comes down to how much money is in your wallet and not whether you're guilty or innocent. Four hundred thousand people, about six out of every ten adults sitting in jail right now, have not yet been convicted of a crime. Their only reason for incarceration? They can't afford freedom. We shouldn't have a two-tiered system of justice like this. Fortunately, there is a growing movement to eliminate the system of money bail as we know it. It is not without opposition. Prison profiteers are screaming bloody murder and spending big lobbying dollars in a desperate attempt to keep the corrupt bail-bonds industry alive. Dozens of states and localities, including Kentucky, Connecticut, and Illinois, have made sweeping changes to their pretrial detention practices. New Jersey, under Governor Chris Christie's leadership, has basically eliminated the use of money bail, instead opting for a risk-based assessment of individual defendants. Six months after passing these key reforms in early 2017, the state's jail population was reduced by 30 percent, to the benefit of mostly black, brown, and poor people.

4. Decriminalize Addiction and Mental Illness

Tom Dart runs the largest mental-healthcare and drug-treatment facility in the country: the Cook County Jail system in Chicago. In nearly every state across the country, jails and prisons hold 1,000 percent more individuals with mental illness than do hospitals. Our prisons and jails have become de facto warehouses for people suffering from mental illness and drug addiction. One out of every three people behind bars suffers from severe mental illness, and rates of addiction and substance-use disorder are extraordinarily high. A cell is no place for someone suffering from mental illness or addiction—this isn't working, and it's not keeping us safe. For that reason, numerous states have set up drug courts, mental-health courts, and veterans courts, and even law-enforcement-assisted diversion programs, which route people away from incarceration and courts and into treatment and other supportive programming.

5. Declassify Low-level Offenses to Keep People Out of Prison

We shouldn't be putting people in prison for low-level crimes, often perpetrated as a result of drug addiction or financial necessity. In

2014, California voters passed a historic ballot initiative that drew the support of allies as unlikely as Newt Gingrich and Jay-Z. Proposition 47 reduced low-level felony crimes—like petty theft and drug possession—and reinvested the savings into community-based treatments that do far more to benefit public safety than sending a bike thief to prison. Two years later, in another election, deep-red Oklahoma passed similar reforms. Research shows that opting for treatment and community programming instead of prison sentences actually makes people less likely to commit future crimes. Over the past decade, dozens of states—both red and blue—have found ways to reduce the number of minor felony crimes, keeping more people out of prison without increasing crime rates.

6. Get Rid of Mandatory Minimum Sentencing

Mandatory minimums are laws that require a specific length of time in prison for a specific crime or possession of a certain quantity of drugs. They began as an attempt to equalize racial disparities in prison sentences but have backfired catastrophically. The problem with mandatory minimums is that sentences are triggered solely by the offense or the quantity of drugs rather than by the actual role or culpability of the individual. Mandatory minimum sentencing handcuffs judges, leaving them unable to recommend appropriate sentences to individual defendants; this has resulted in the unjust and lengthy incarceration of tens of thousands of individuals. A better approach would be to "let judges judge" by restoring evidence-based discretion. In 2017, as part of a far-reaching package of reforms aimed at removing Louisiana's dubious distinction of being the nation's leading incarcerator, Governor John Bel Edwards signed a bill that repealed most of Louisiana's mandatory-minimum drug-sentencing laws. Dozens of other states have made minor reforms to their mandatory-minimum sentencing practices, but much more must be done, especially in the federal system, where nearly half of individuals sentenced to prison are serving time for drug offenses.

7. Abolish Solitary Confinement

On any given day, nearly one hundred thousand people are locked alone in tiny cells for twenty-three and sometimes twenty-four hours, with little to no human contact. Solitary confinement shouldn't be allowed in any prison or jail in America, yet we turn our heads and let the inhumane practice carry on. Some leaders have taken action. President Obama issued a historic executive order to limit the use of solitary confinement in federal prisons, banning the practice for juveniles and setting strict limits on the amount of time individuals can be placed in solitary for disciplinary infractions. Nearly a dozen states have curtailed the practice, but it is still far too common.

8. Increase Access to Prison Education and Visitation

The most effective way to prepare individuals for a successful return to their communities is to ensure that our prisons have strong education programming and a deep commitment to family visitation. These two simple tools have been shown to dramatically enhance an individual's success and stability post-prison. I have had the pleasure of visiting one of the most programmed prisons in the country, San Quentin, located just thirty minutes outside of San Francisco. With access to volunteers, family members, and some of the best programming in the country, incarcerated men in San Quentin are among the most emotionally and spiritually intelligent people I have come across. If we must have prisons in this country, we need more of them to emulate the positive features of San Quentin.

9. Ease Collateral Consequences and Reentry, Commit to Jobs

Some 70 million to 100 million people in the United States—more than a quarter of all adults—have a criminal record, and every year an additional six hundred thousand men and women return home from prison. Upon their return home, many are denied the right to vote, barred from business licensing, stripped of parental rights, and face discrimination in employment, housing, and access to finance. It is tragic but not surprising that 60 to 75 percent of all people who return home from prison end up incarcerated again within five years. When someone leaves physical prison, it is cruel and foolish to keep them locked in an economic and social prison. We all have a vested interest in ensuring that people who have served their time are able to successfully find meaningful work and careers, stable housing, and participate in full economic, social, and civic life. To do so, we will need corporations to take the injustice head on—making a commitment to hiring and a second chance. Companies like Dave's Killer Bread, the number one organic-bread brand in the United States, have embedded second-chance employment into their DNA. Now owned by Flowers Foods, one of the most conservative companies in America, Dave's Killer Bread and its foundation have doubled down on their investment, working with other business leaders to highlight best practices and build a robust community of companies invested in the success of returning citizens.

10. Restore Voting Rights

The pernicious effects of over-incarceration may be most egregious and damaging when we examine the impact on our democracy. In dozens of states across the country, a felony conviction can lead to a lengthy and sometimes lifetime ban from voting or running for political office. At this writing, three key states—Florida, Iowa, and Virginia—bar individuals with felony convictions from voting for life. In Florida, nearly 10 percent of the adult population cannot vote because of a prior felony conviction. And while the fight to restore voting rights has been overwhelmingly supported by Democrats and objectively roadblocked by Republicans in nearly every state in the union, there is a bipartisan movement in Florida, led by a formerly homeless black organizer named Desmond Meade and a white conservative named Neil Volz, to overturn the state's lifetime ban on voting for people with felony convictions via a ballot initiative in the 2018 election.

END THE ADDICTION CRISIS

In late January 2017, I flew to Charleston, West Virginia, to gather stories for a special report on coal miners in a post-Trump-victory era that would air on both *Anderson Cooper 360°* and *The Messy Truth*.

I've been to West Virginia countless times, so the gray geometry of used-up land you see when you approach from the sky—quarries and denuded mountains—isn't a surprise to me. This time, however, I got a wake-up call on my way from the airport to the city. My cabdriver that day was a young white guy, taking online university classes when he wasn't driving. He had a lot to say.

As we wound around curves and jerked to stops, we could see the city of Charleston on the horizon. There was the capitol building, the Kanawha River, rolling hills, and bare trees. The cab rumbled over potholes and bumps. The driver and I were in the middle of talking about one of his classes on political theory, when he got suddenly serious.

"You know how they say that religion is the opiate of the masses? Well, not around here." He paused, letting out a dry chuckle. "Opioids are the opiates of the masses. They done cut Jesus clean out of the picture. They're about to put Jesus out of business. They want their heaven right here on earth! Or they want to go to heaven right now. And some of 'em don't care which." He held my gaze in the rearview mirror, challenging me, it seemed, to report on that.

WEST VIRGINIA HAS BEEN HIT particularly hard by the opioid epidemic. In late 2016, *The Washington Post* embarked on a series of reports about "opiate orphans" and the high cost of these drugs on the poor and disenfranchised in West Virginia. One of these kids was seventeen-year-old Zaine. Zaine and his sisters woke one morning to a quiet house, the door to their parents' bedroom door locked. He would eventually bust down the door and tumble over his father's cold body. His mother's was nearby. They were too far gone for CPR.

Unfortunately, this has become a familiar story.

The *Los Angeles Times* reported that in 2016, the small town of Huntington, West Virginia (population 50,000), suffered twenty-six overdoses in just a few hours. First responders came across the bodies of seven people overdosed on heroin in one house. Dispatcher orders blared all day, sending police officers and firefighters rappelling across the city, coming across overdosed men and women in gas-station bathrooms, Family Dollar stores, Burger King parking lots, and slumped across steering wheels in traffic. Only a few made it to hospitals. The rest went straight to the morgue.

Opioid addiction has become a nationwide epidemic, with both rural and urban poor white communities among the hardest hit. As New Jersey Republican governor Chris Christie stated in his 2017 State of the State address, "Our friends are dying, our neighbors are dying. Our co-workers are dying. Our children are dying, every day, in numbers we can no longer afford to ignore."

Opioid addiction has nothing to do with an emotional or moral weakness. Many people get addicted to painkillers first through legitimate doctor's orders. They eventually switch to heroin when the prescription runs out. Heroin, it turns out, is cheaper to buy and easier to acquire than prescription drugs. Indeed, the initial addiction to painkillers often has nothing to do with a back-alley drug deal. The same white coat who prescribes amoxicillin for your daughter's ear infection could fill a scrip for any number of opioids.

That's how it went down for the older brother of one of the guys on whom I based Bryce Shoemaker, the struggling conservative I described earlier in this book. Let's call him "Big Bill" Shoemaker. His knees are shot from the combination of his halcyon days as a teenaged athlete and then from his lifetime of factory work. Every few steps forward feel like walking across broken glass. That's how he describes it over beers to anyone who will listen. Most of his life has been spent in various degrees of pain. Alcohol helps dull the ache, but he's no alcoholic. He went to the doctor and came home with a prescription for hydrocodone. That did more than dull the pain—bliss!

Beyond the temporary relief, however, Bill feels nauseous and vomits nearly every day. He now has a lumbering gait, not because of his bad knees but because of his distended gut. He jokes with pals that his body has no problem puking but he has trouble in the bathroom. He has trouble breathing, too—he's always short of breath. He doesn't remember names as well as he used to. He has violent mood swings. He vaguely remembers pushing somebody. A stranger? A loved one? Still, the pills give him something he's never had before: pain relief.

The opioid problem in America is pervasive and has reached a fever pitch. Accidental drug overdoses now outpace car accidents as the number one cause of accidental death in the United States. Doctors recklessly prescribe opioids, whether it's for a concussion or a herniated disc, a twisted ankle or surgery recovery. They are overprescribed.

People get hooked either due to chronic pain and not having any other option or because leftover pills taken recreationally or to treat minor pain have led to chemical dependence. Opioids chemically alter the brain and make people physiologically vulnerable and dependent on the drug. And while biological predispositions account for nearly half of one's likelihood of addiction, addiction does not discriminate along socioeconomic lines. Indeed, it was ultimately determined that fentanyl, an opioid one hundred times more powerful than heroin, was what killed Prince.

Over the last few months, I have returned to Appalachia to learn more and report for CNN. The sprawling fields showed tufts of life creeping up from the earth. The drives through town remind me of that cab ride. On the country horizon, I imagined the overdose number ticking up a digit with no end in sight. I know from family experience that addiction and poverty are not choices. Whether someone faces death in the Family Dollar of suburbia or on Lenox Avenue in New York, whether from a bad batch of heroin or from years of painkiller dependency, whether by one fatal dose or from countless years of substance use, we need good solutions to these devastating problems.

After Prince died, I cast around looking for ways that I could help, things I could do that would honor my friend's memory and do good in the world in a way that I know he would have approved of. In 2017, I joined forces with Newt Gingrich and Patrick Kennedy to create an advocacy group called Advocates for Opioid Recovery. As unlikely as our alliance might seem on paper, all three of us are fired by a personal passion to find solutions. I do this work for Prince. Kennedy himself is in recovery from a substance-abuse disorder. Gingrich has had addiction issues touch his family. And, even more improbable, we are funded in part by pharmaceutical entrepreneurs who want to shake up the pain-research establishment and find safer, smarter products that help people overcome addiction and get off drugs.

So what can be done? How do we save one another? Here are some solutions:

1. End the "Detox and Die" Model

Here's an ever-increasing cycle: People go into detox, get a little bit better, then they come out and inevitably turn back to the drugs. But because the drugs have been out of their system for a long-enough time, their tolerance has dropped and the dosage that their bodies had become accustomed to often kills them. People who are addicted need better solutions, and their survival depends on doctors seeing and treating opioid addiction as a chronic brain disease. One of those solutions is medication-assisted treatment (MAT), which is a drug-treatment regimen that can help fend off the physiological dependencies associated with opioid addiction and give the brain a chance to heal itself. MAT is a proven method toward recovery, with low relapse rates. It's what nearly every medical expert and drug-policy researcher who examines this problem recommends. The evidence shows that MAT is safer, less expensive, and less socially and economically damning than abstinence-only programs, therapy alone, or cold-turkey detox treatments.

Multiple studies have shown that medication-assisted treatments are essential to effective long-term recovery, by reducing cravings and the risk of fatal overdose and increasing abstinence and time in treatment. A multicenter clinical trial published in *The New England Journal of Medicine* found that buprenorphine reduced the craving to use an opiate by roughly 50 percent and increased the odds of not taking an opiate by about 3.5 times. Fewer people die if they have MAT behind them. If we want to end opioid addiction, we must get healthcare providers, medical professionals, politicians, and the law to treat addiction like the disease it is.

2. Make This Lifesaving Drug Readily Available

There is a short-term fix to the growing wave of accidental-overdose deaths that must be made widely available to anyone who needs it. Naloxone is an injection or nasal spray that immediately blocks the effects of the drug and literally stops an overdose in its tracks. In the hands of a friend, first responder, or community health worker, it can be lifesaving. Communities across the country are implementing programs to distribute naloxone and preventing thousands of deaths.

3. Treat People in the Criminal-Justice System

Thanks to the disastrous war on drugs, our jails, prisons, and courtrooms are full of individuals who are incarcerated or under correctional supervision as a result of their addiction to drugs. Too many prosecutors, judges, and prison wardens are still under the misconception that drug abuse is a moral, behavioral flaw, as opposed to a serious disease requiring medical treatment. We need to rid the criminal-justice system of anti-scientific harmful biases against those struggling with substance-use disorders. Currently, only 11 percent of all inmates with substance-use disorders receive any form of treatment during their incarceration, despite the high potential of treatment with medicine to reduce both recidivism and criminal-justice costs. Offering incarcerated individuals and those who are on probation, parole, or drug-court programs pharmacological treatment and counseling for opiate dependence decreases the likelihood of relapse, overdose, future crime, and even HIV infection. It also dramatically increases the likelihood of remaining in long-term drug treatment after release.

4. Encourage Insurer Support

Insurance companies should pay for effective treatment. They should enforce mental-health and addiction parity across all health-care coverage and break down insurance barriers to covering addiction treatment that actually works. Insurance companies can do this by requiring adequate provider networks and treatment coverage. They can offer incentives to plans that comply with parity laws and those with improved treatment outcomes. In October 2016, the New York attorney general's office pushed Cigna to make a national decision to totally eliminate preauthorization for medication-assisted treatment. We need more of that kind of action. It is unacceptable to discourage an effective treatment that can save lives.

5. Train Medical Practitioners, First Responders, and Community Service Providers

We need to train more doctors and nurse practitioners to deal with this crisis. Only 8 percent of the medical schools in America have mandatory addiction-medicine training, and only 36 percent even offer it as an elective. All medical students and currently licensed professionals should be trained in medication-assisted treatment.

6. Decriminalize Addiction, Period

If dealing with a crisis this big doesn't bring us together, shame on us. But also shame on us if we stop with opioid addiction only. Earlier heroin-addiction crises in the 1970s and the crack cocaine–addiction crises during the 1980s and '90s did not result in sane or wise policy. Instead, we tried to arrest our way out of those problems. The face of those crises was black. We now are faced with this bizarre situation where Attorney General Sessions wants to double down on incarceration as an answer for the epidemic while

Trump and others are suggesting a more clinical and compassionate approach to opioids. It's hard to see this double standard as anything other than racially biased. Compassion and medical treatment are absolutely the right response to the disease of addiction—but they must not be reserved only for white victims. Funerals are funerals. Addiction is addiction. We cannot work to save white rural communities while continuing the destruction of black urban ones. We should all work together to use this moment to change the way that we deal with addiction overall.

TWENTY-FIRST-CENTURY JOBS: HIGH TECH

We spend most of our time in politics arguing about which party has picked the right set of bad guys to rail against. The Democrats want more oversight and controls on Wall Street; the Republicans believe the Washington establishment is stymieing employment with too many business rules and corporate taxes. No matter which side wins, Americans might still lose—because both sides are missing the larger threat. Neither D.C. nor Wall Street poses the most serious danger to American workers, despite what you might be led to believe. That peril actually comes from an entirely different set of elites—in Silicon Valley.

Technology is great for consumers. But it can be bad for workers, who can find their entire industry disrupted by an app, their entire skill set rendered irrelevant by a robot, or their entire profession replaced by computers using artificial intelligence. This happened on a small scale to my co-workers and friends at *The Jackson Sun* when we got our new printing press. In the age of the robot, an almost inconceivable number of jobs soon will become obsolete. The rise of machines has eliminated millions of manufacturing jobs in the United States over the past decades, and middle-class service workers in finance, retail, food, and transportation may be next.

As new technologies upend and disrupt more industries, all American communities are facing a serious job-creation challenge—in red states and in blue states, in big cities and small towns. Preparing all workers for the coming turbulence is a brutally difficult challenge. Workers and students who are female, or those who are nonwhite and non-Asian, are most at risk of being left behind.* Neither party has all the answers; few politicians seem to even have their heads around the issue. If we want to prevent widespread poverty far beyond what we face today, the time to act is now.

My own involvement in trying to open up the tech sector to all people, not only the Silicon Valley elite, was initiated in an unusual manner: A rock star made me do it.

I was with Prince at his home in Minneapolis shortly after a jury exonerated the neighborhood vigilante who shot to death seventeen-year-old Trayvon Martin. Everyone gathered there was upset; it was a watershed moment in the movement for black lives.

Prince said, "Why is it that when someone sees a black kid wearing a hoodie, they automatically think, 'There goes a thug.' But if they see a white kid wearing a hoodie? That could be Mark Zuckerberg." He looked around at all of us in the room that night. "Why is that?"

Prince didn't do small talk. He was the kind of person who always cut to the chase and spoke directly to the heart of the matter. So many great things in my life came out of talking with Prince. When Prince posed the question about the significance of Trayvon's hoodie, I gave the only answer that came to my mind: "It's racism," I said.

"Maybe you're right, Van," he said. "Or maybe we just haven't

---

* According to a 2016 Gizmodo survey that used 2015 diversity data, only 5 percent of hires at major tech companies were non-Asian people of color (Hispanic, black, two or more races) and 16 percent of hires at these same companies were women. This resulted despite big tech companies dedicating millions of dollars to diversity efforts.

created enough black Mark Zuckerbergs. Maybe we should focus on that."

His answer blew me away. Prince wasn't red or blue: He was purple. He had the magical ability to dream up songs that everyone could dance to. People dance to his hits at Republican weddings and Democratic weddings, too. People of all races and ages love his music. The same mind that created musical performances also created social programs. Again and again, he would leap beyond traditional partisan thinking to entirely fresh solutions. That night, out of talking about Trayvon, we essentially came up with the seeds for #YesWeCode.

As I mentioned earlier, Prince helped launch #YesWeCode at the 2014 Essence Festival in New Orleans at a concert attended by fifty thousand people. My co-founders—Amy Henderson and Cheryl Contee—and I took the ball from there and ran with it. Among other things, #YesWeCode sponsored hackathons across the country. The idea was to let urban youth experiment with using technology to solve their everyday problems. We went on the road to test out Prince's thought experiment: What might happen for teens and children in hoodies—or whatever the urban uniform would be next—if we trained them in computer science?

According to the Department of Labor, by 2020 there will be more than 1.4 million computer-science jobs in the tech sector. In that time, only four hundred thousand students are expected to graduate from a four-year university or college with a STEM (science, technology, engineering, or math) degree. That could leave an astounding one million jobs unfilled in the next few years. #YesWe-Code set out to try to put a dent in those numbers. We saw an opportunity to change the odds for success in STEM by encouraging students from disadvantaged or nontraditional backgrounds to learn coding. Major tech giants jumped in to help, including Facebook, Google, Salesforce, Qeyno Labs, Hidden Genius Project, Black Girls Code, Ford STEAM Lab, Detroit Labs, and more.

But how was I going to get the kids on board? With any audience, a new issue must be framed properly. I soon came up with an idea for getting the attention of African American youth. It would be slightly risky, but I decided to try out my pitch when I spoke to an auditorium of mostly black students in New Orleans.

As I stood at the podium, I could feel the room buzzing with teen restlessness. Without saying a word, I held up my cellphone, high over my head. The room quieted down, and I said, "I only have three questions. But they just might change your life.

"Number one: How many of you have one of these?" Meaning a smartphone. Every kid in the room raised a hand. Some even raised their own devices.

"Number two: How many of you have ever downloaded an app?" Everyone raised a hand again. By now some of them were snickering. Where's this old guy going with this?

"Number three: How many of you have ever *uploaded* an app?" Not a single hand went up. "I mean, seriously. How many of you have ever built your *own* app? And then uploaded it?" Nothing. Silence from the students.

"You know why?" I said. "Because you're suckers. That's why." I let that sink in for a few seconds. Glancing around, I noticed some teachers frowning, looking skeptical. Did this guy show up to berate their kids about always being glued to their phones? They didn't know where I was going with this, either.

I kept going. "Every time you move your thumbs around on one of those smart screens, you're making someone else tons of money. Someone you don't even know. Someone who doesn't care about you." I paused for effect. "Black people using their fingers to make money for other people? We used to call that picking cotton."

By that point I had everyone's attention, but the adults in the room looked like they were on the verge of a coronary.

"That's right. Picking cotton," I said. "But I don't want you to be digital cotton-pickers in the information age. I don't want you sitting here all day, creating billions of dollars of economic value for people who see you only as clicks or eyeballs—not even as full human beings. We already went through that. I want you to be the makers, the owners, the builders of this new century." By now the restlessness had transformed into nods and the low hum of whispered excitement. I had them.

"I want you to write your own code. I want you to build your own apps and upload them. Who wants to learn how to do *that*?"

Every single hand in that room flew up. Even the adults, who'd looked skeptical a few moments ago, were smiling now.

I gave dozens of speeches like that one all over the country to promote #YesWeCode. We got teens to sign up, and we quickly learned that students from nontraditional backgrounds had a profound hunger to learn computer science.

#YesWeCode now runs the biggest scholarship fund in the United States to help people from low-opportunity backgrounds gain access to computer-science education. And we are not alone. Fortunately, there are charitable organizations, companies, and cities working hard to close the gap. There are numerous other nonprofits making a difference; I list many in Appendix 2.

Through #YesWeCode, I've gotten a chance to work with Silicon Valley's top firms. None are perfect. But all are responding to the need for change, and I applaud their growing commitment to inclusion and diversity. Here are some examples of the strides they're making:

Google recently partnered with Howard University, one of the nation's most prominent historically black universities, to immerse young black computer-science majors in the company.

HP Inc. has created one of the most diverse boards in corporate America while diversifying its workforce and increasing the number of women at the executive level. Among other things, it created a powerful media campaign called "We'll Be in Touch," to raise awareness around ingrained biases within the tech hiring process.

Facebook understands that diversity is imperative for its future growth. As their Global Director of Diversity, Maxine Williams, stated: "If we don't get it right, we risk losing relevance in an incredibly diverse world." Facebook has increased efforts to recruit more underrepresented minorities through initiatives like Facebook University, an internship program for college freshmen interested in computer science, and Facebook Academy, a summer-internship program for Bay Area high school students from underserved communities.

To address and eliminate gender discrimination, Salesforce has conducted salary assessments in the company to focus on pay parity at all levels on an ongoing basis. They've implemented nonprofit partnerships in order to drive more STEM trainees of color to Salesforce and have successfully launched new apprenticeship models for low-opportunity youth.

In addition to the beautiful work done in the tech business sector, I've been encouraged by sweeping efforts in cities across America that echo our mission at #YesWeCode. In Chicago, a city often in the news for its high levels of violent crime, we have the first public school district in the nation to identify computer science as a core graduation requirement. Recognizing Chicago's success and forward thinking, the Obama White House launched a national Computer Science For All (CS4All) initiative in 2016. New York City set a goal to ensure that all New Yorkers, regardless of income, have access to reliable broadband Internet by 2025. Under the leadership of the city's new chief technology officer, Miguel Gamino, New York now has more than one million subscribers to their LinkNYC program, the world's largest and fastest free public Wi-Fi network. Pittsburgh is vying to become the "Silicon Valley of the East," and that includes a "Roadmap for Inclusive Innovation," which focuses on addressing the digital divide, using open data to improve the quality of life for city residents, advancing clean technologies, and investments in immigrant- and minority-owned tech businesses.

Smaller cities in red states, like New Orleans and Austin, are creating tech initiatives that are cognizant of including their cities' cultural heritages and community involvement. Louisiana's Digital Interactive Media and Software Development tax incentive reflects the growing number of companies claiming the credits and growing the state's tech environment, increasing from $377,000 in 2009 to $15 million in 2014. Current New Orleans mayor Mitch Landrieu launched the Digital Equity Challenge to come up with ways to connect underserved New Orleanians—including low-income, minority, elderly, and disabled residents—to technology. The city is advocating for community leaders and tech companies to propose innovative ideas to solve the technology-opportunity gap and make New Orleans the next great tech city. Much like New Orleans, Austin is driving its tech boom through smart government incentives. With its vibrant arts culture and university-rich workforce, Austin was ranked the number one tech destination in 2017 as a more affordable, talent-rich alternative to San Francisco.

How can we come together to spread the education and training that Americans need to succeed in the emerging digital economy? First, parents and neighbors need to encourage the youth, unemployed people, and underemployed people in our lives—especially those who would have nontraditional backgrounds for tech—to try STEM plus arts education and stick with it. Second, voters should support candidates who are dedicated to increasing STEM plus arts education in our public schools and universities. Third, investors should back would-be tech entrepreneurs who are female, nonwhite, or based in small towns or rural areas. Their firms may well spot a different set of problems, creating value in unexpected places.

But the biggest game changer of all is one we have yet to discuss: high-quality "bootcamp" training programs to rapidly accelerate the education of would-be computer coders.

We need to think beyond college as we imagine an American workforce that can thrive in the twenty-first century. Yes, college is important. But graduation rates are not moving fast enough to keep up with economic demand in the United States. The most prominent example of this is in the tech sector; the demand for developers is growing exponentially. But the one area that tech has fallen into traditional ways is by relying on college graduates to supply its workforce. As a result, the pool of available coders doesn't have enough people—and the people don't have enough diversity when it comes to race and gender. The way to both deepen and broaden the pool is to accelerate access to a new kind of educational opportunity: bootcamp training programs.

A form of nontraditional workforce development, coding bootcamps are full-time intensive programs. They ideally take those who are new to coding and transform them into employable software developers. These training programs produce qualified coders in fewer than six months. There were more than two thousand coding-bootcamp graduates in 2013. In 2016, we saw a 725 percent growth in bootcamp graduates, to 17,966. The bootcamp industry is primed to close the unfilled jobs in the tech industry with amazing effectiveness and efficiency.

Despite the efficiency and the effectiveness of the coding-bootcamp model, it's not perfect. Good ones don't exist everywhere. With a price tag of fifteen thousand dollars to attend a coding bootcamp, many can't afford the entry fee. Also, bootcamp staffing generally reflects the current demographics of the tech sector. As a result, the learning environments there sometimes mirror the STEM learning environments, which can feel unwelcoming to women of all colors and men of color. The key is for bootcamps to teach in more-creative inclusive ways and to engage with multicultural communities. Coding bootcamps still have a great opportunity to get it right. Details of coding bootcamps can be found in Appendix 2.

WHEN I MET COLLETTE, SHE was a stay-at-home mom. She was a self-taught coder who loved the craft, like someone passionate about learning a new language and culture. Collette had been studying on her own for two years, using free tutorials she'd found online. She had basic skills but lacked the level of expertise for a career in tech. To her, coding was a hobby. She didn't know how to move forward. Through #YesWeCode, Collette got an opportunity to attend a coding academy near her home, and we helped to offset the cost of her childcare while she was in classes. Bootcamp is called that for a reason—it's an intense and often grueling experience. #YesWeCode's staff provided community support, advice, and advocacy for her when the going got tough.

As a part of the #YesWeCode Coding Corps, Collette will be the first to tell you that attending the bootcamp not only expanded her coding skills exponentially but also broadened her professional network, something that's invaluable in the tech sector. After graduating, Collette found a full-time position in a medium-sized tech company. In fewer than nine months, her life was transformed: She went from being a full-time mom (a hard job, and one that's unpaid) to making ninety-five thousand dollars annually. Best of all, Collette's self-confidence has gone through the roof.

For the first time in decades, technology has allowed for Americans to jump directly out of poverty and into a growing profession, with the chance to earn a good living and even to become an entrepreneur. There is employable talent out there in our youth and minority communities, as yet untapped. To soar, people just need financial support, a community that they can rely on, and a professional network that they can activate. The tech industry needs leaders like Collette, and #YesWeCode and our allies are working to create more opportunities for nontraditional techies like her. With #YesWeCode, it's not a pipe dream. I know what's possible; I have seen it with my own eyes.

All of this hope and help grew out of one conversation with Prince, on a night when supporters of Trayvon Martin's family were deep in mourning. Rather than give in to bitterness, Prince helped transform a community's pain into purpose. My hope is that everyone will follow his example—and search within for solutions that unify and heal.

TWENTY-FIRST-CENTURY JOBS: CLEAN TECH

In April of 2013, I found myself in St. Louis, Missouri. Thousands of people were gathered to protest outside the headquarters of Peabody Energy, the world's largest coal company. The United Mine Workers of America had planned the demonstration and had invited me to be one of the speakers at the rally. Everywhere you looked you saw coal miners—some still active and some gray-haired retirees—and their families. Most of them wore caps to shield their faces from the sun and white T-shirts that said "Peabody Promised, Peabody Lied." Joining them, but wearing red shirts, were members of the Communications Workers of America. Other unions came, as well, in a great show of solidarity. Over the loudspeaker, the classic American union song "Which Side Are You On?" rang out. Poignantly, the lyrics ask: "Tell me what you gonna do?/ When there's one law for the rulers/And one law for the ruled."

Six years earlier and facing a corporate financial crisis, Peabody Energy had created a spin-off company called the Patriot Coal Corporation. Peabody then off-loaded most of its worker pensions and health-insurance plans—dumping them into the new, under-capitalized company. When Patriot filed for Chapter 11 bankruptcy, the coal miners saw it as failure by design: Peabody wanted Patriot to fail so the company could renege on the promises it made to its loyal workers. The printed signs that some of the workers carried summed it up perfectly: PEABODY CREATED PATRIOT TO FAIL. PATRIOT'S GREED KILLS. ARE YOU NEXT? Others held up signs they had made themselves. One particularly heartbreaking sign displayed a photo of an elderly couple and a list of the couple's ailments: CANCER, BRAIN ANEURYSM, DIABETES, HIGH BLOOD PRESSURE.

The miners and workers surrounding me were part of a long and noble tradition. And I very much supported their cause. As a former Obama official and a prominent environmentalist, I was there to help shame Peabody and Patriot—and stand up for the workers as best I could. I was, however, one of only a few black men there. And in a crowd of working-class white folks wearing jeans and T-shirts, I stuck out like a sore thumb in my blue blazer and red tie. When it came to the ballot box, I probably wasn't on their side. Regardless, on that day and in that context, I knew which side I was on—theirs. One hundred percent.

But why was I the only Democrat with a national platform there to support the miners? We liberals claim to fight for downtrodden Americans, but it didn't look like it that day in St. Louis. In my view, it is unconscionable to ask people to go down into dark, dangerous holes every day, risking their lungs and lives to keep our lights turned on, and then ignore their needs. I hope we decide to leave more coal in the ground, but regardless we have to honor the promises we made to the people who put their bodies on the line when we were busy taking it out.

The rally drew to a close and the time of the march neared. We bowed our heads in prayer, then moved like a strong, slow-flowing river toward our destination, the U.S. Bankruptcy Court. People held up more signs: WE ONLY WANT WHAT WE WORKED FOR, PEABODY! SHAME ON YOU, PATRIOT! BROKEN PROMISES THREATEN

PEOPLE'S LIVES. This all felt familiar to me. I felt good about being here.

One thing bothered me, though. Everyone was so damn quiet. I knew they were angry and wounded. And they had every right to make themselves heard. Hurt people holler. So how come they weren't getting loud?

I figured they probably just needed a little nudge. My voice is loud, and I don't mind using it. I've been the hype man at plenty of protests, so I rose to the occasion—shouting one of my old-school chants from Oakland:

"Ain't no power like the power of the people, 'cause the power of the people don't stop! Say what?"

I waited for people to join in, to reply to my call, but no one did. They didn't make a sound. In fact, they barely seemed to notice.

Maybe they were just shy or needed another nudge. I shouted even louder this time, cupping my hands around my mouth:

"Ain't no power like the power of the people, 'cause the power of the people don't stop! Say what?"

Crickets.

I was starting to feel a little stupid. Confused. Why weren't they responding? Didn't they want me here?

I felt someone next to me and turned. It was the wife of one of the miners, a small woman. She touched my elbow and motioned me closer. I leaned down toward her.

"Don't be offended," she said. "They can't."

"They can't what?"

She gently tapped the center of her chest.

The penny dropped for me. I got it.

They couldn't shout. They couldn't chant.

After years of breathing bad air down in the bowels of the earth, their lungs wouldn't let them. Serious respiratory ailments, including black lung disease, made it a struggle for some of the men just to walk down the street. A few were pulling small oxygen tanks along with them.

I don't think I'll ever forget the lesson I learned in that moment. I had flown in to support a cause I knew was important. I wanted badly to help, and I thought I understood the issues. But I didn't fully get it. These men and their wives were fighting for their lives. Many of them were desperately ill—and they had gotten sick working in Peabody's mines. They had taken home modest paychecks in exchange for a promise of secure pensions and lifetime healthcare. Peabody had swindled them out of those pensions and even placed their medical coverage at risk. Without access to top-notch doctors, many of the men who were marching right next to me would die. Plain and simple. But Peabody— a mega-profitable energy company—didn't give a damn. To save a few bucks, the executives in charge were perfectly willing to abandon these men to their fates. I realized that the fight to protect sick and retired miners, along with their wives and widows, was a life-or-death struggle. It was as serious and consequential as any battle I had ever taken on in urban America.

The coal-mining industry is a target of progressive activism because the burning of fossil fuels disrupts earth's climate. But we all must acknowledge that we have personally benefitted from the labor of those miners whose courage and skill have undergirded America's economy for generations. A changing economy need not leave these workers behind. We need programs to train active miners, giving them the skills needed in new industries. We need a just transition, a responsible evolution.

The good news is this: It's possible. We can help heal the bodies of the coal miners. We can work to save their pensions. We can help heal the land. And we can create a new, clean energy economy that is better for the people and the planet.

In fact, the Dream Corps worked in solidarity with a broad-based coalition and won the battle to secure healthcare benefits for twenty thousand coal miners in spring of 2017. We are now engaged in the battle to save their pensions, too. We can also redeem and save the land, which has suffered due to our addiction to fossil fuels.

There is a model we can follow. When big changes hit, America's government has a long history of stepping up with "transition assistance." In 1944, the GI Bill helped veterans transition home from World War II. Starting in the late 1980s, the Base Realignment and Closure (BRAC) process helped communities absorb the shock when military bases were closed. Over the years, America's government has offered "trade adjustment assistance" to help workers affected by the outsourcing of jobs overseas. The transition away from a predominantly fossil-fuel economy to a cleaner mix of energy sources is also monumental. It will require adequate investment to protect and respect the workers who powered our nation to this point.

WHILE I AM NEW TO the front lines in coal country, the issues involved in the transition to a cleaner, greener economy are not new to me. In 2009, during my brief tenure as the special adviser for green jobs at the White House, the Democrats in Congress had passed an emergency stimulus bill amounting to 787 billion dollars. Eighty billion dollars of that was earmarked for green and clean solutions. That would translate to billions of dollars for solar panels, energy-efficient retrofits of buildings, smart batteries, wind turbines, and more. It was my job to help coordinate the efforts of the dozen departments and agencies that would receive parts of this 80 billion dollars. I was tasked with making sure the money was spent efficiently and effectively. But in the back of my mind,

I was worried. Unless we planned properly, a transition to solar and wind power, and away from fossil fuels like coal, might decimate entire towns and counties.

I asked my superiors for a meeting and revealed to them my secret desire to flood Appalachia with green investments. I argued that it was morally right, economically feasible, and politically smart to make sure we were investing more than we were taking in a region that had already given so much to America. After all, in some ways Appalachia has long been a sacrifice zone, asked to blow up its mountains and to poison its streams with the runoff from coal mining. I saw the opportunity to turn a center of local suffering into a showcase for global solutions. Why not spare mountaintops slated for removal and outfit them with wind turbines? Why not reclaim the land that had been ruined by mining activities, returning it to its natural state or redeveloping it for other commercial uses that would reinvigorate local economies?

I was fired up and ready to go, but it was less than delicately pointed out to me that we had no clear statutory authority to launch a green crusade against Appalachian poverty. Congress had not passed any such law, and it would be illegal to play favorites with stimulus dollars, no matter how poor or deserving the region. I argued, however, that there was nothing to stop the administration from taking steps to ensure that dollars already headed for the region were well spent. I pointed out that there was an organization already on the books to help Appalachia—the Appalachian Regional Commission. Founded in 1965, the ARC had a mandate to look for ways to help people in the region move out of poverty. I proposed that we consult with the ARC when considering ways to spend the 80 billion dollars.

My argument prevailed, and I was granted permission to work with the ARC, among other regional entities. Soon after, we held a meeting with the head of the ARC and officials from numerous departments and agencies in positions to dispense funds. As we went around the table and everyone explained their ideas for spending in ways that would benefit the country but also Appalachia, the ARC director looked more and more pleased. We had everything we needed to make a tremendous difference for people who had been forgotten for too long. Unfortunately, I resigned my position within two weeks of that meeting, so I never got to bring that vision to life. But my ideas lived on through others in the Obama administration: In 2016, it put forward the POWER+ Plan. The proposal—an acronym for Partnerships for Opportunity and Workforce and Economic Revitalization—would have specifically sent help to Appalachian communities that were getting left behind because of the rapidly changing energy market. The Republican Congress never funded the idea, though.

That said, dreams die hard. I continue to fight for a future in which well-paid work to heal the land can also have a healing effect on people and our economy. The global demand for coal is slowing, and coal from Wyoming costs a fraction of the coal from Appalachia. It's time to focus on creating twenty-first-century opportunities in coal country.

OUR MINERS AREN'T THE ONLY ones who need help transitioning to a clean-energy economy. Poor black and brown communities live on the front lines of some of the worst pollution in America. They have always been hit first and worst by the pollution-based economy; they shouldn't benefit last and least as we shift to greener and cleaner solutions.

Take Flint, Michigan, much in the news for lead in its drinking water.

Because the city ran into budget troubles in 2013, Michigan's governor, Rick Snyder, appointed a special emergency-management council to take over the city. One of the initiatives that the council instituted to cut costs was to switch the Flint water supply from Detroit's system to the local Flint River.

But the water from the Flint River was toxic. How toxic? It rusted engine parts at a local GM plant. After just four months, the plant decided to switch back to the Detroit system for its water. But the residents of Flint had no such option. The women, men, and children of Flint—42 percent of whom live below the poverty line and most of whom are black—had to drink, cook with, and bathe in water that could corrode metal.

Denettra Brown and her now-four-year-old son, Dana Brock, are representative of the problems. Among other health issues, little Dana has had five severe seizures this year alone, swollen and infected tonsils, tooth decay, and breathing problems. A sleep specialist informed Denettra that Dana's breathing had stopped eighty-three times in a single hour of monitoring. But it's not just drinking the water that has impacted Dana; it's bathing in it, as well. Once Denettra gave Dana a shower after he wet his pants. Within two minutes of being exposed to the toxic water in that shower, his delicate skin started to crack and blister and bleed. It's no surprise that a sample of the water from Denettra's bathtub was found to contain sixteen parts per billion (ppb) of lead. Understand this: For federal regulators, fifteen ppb is a threshold, the point at which a water system must take action to protect public health.

Or let's talk about Nakiya Wakes and her family. Optimistic about making a new start in life, Nakiya and her two children moved to Flint right when the water source was switched: 2014. Soon thereafter, she became pregnant. Five weeks into her pregnancy, however, she miscarried. But while being checked at the hospital, her doctors detected another heartbeat. She had actually been pregnant with twins! Confident that this one was going to make it, Nakiya began to buy clothes and supplies. But at the beginning of her second trimester, Nakiya miscarried again. Waiting in her mail when she came home from the hospital that second time was a notice from the city of Flint, warning residents of something they had understood for months: It was unsafe for pregnant women to drink the water.

It should go without saying that all women should have access to water that does not cause them to miscarry. This idea is one that can and should unite environmentalist liberals and pro-life conservatives. That's a coalition waiting to happen. We can't be so eager to cut costs or so panicked about "job-killing regulations" that we enact child-killing deregulation.

I asked Michigan Democrat congressman Dan Kildee, "If ISIS came up with a strategy to poison ten thousand American children, what would happen?"

He said, "Congress would act within twenty-four hours." But to this day, precious little has been done by the government at any level. Instead, it's local citizens who are showing us the way.

This tragedy has brought the best out in many people—including the mostly white guys in some of Michigan's labor unions. Volunteers from plumbers' unions—mostly Flint's United Association Local 370, but also others from around the state—have risen to the challenge, visiting more than forty-five hundred homes in Flint and totaling more than ten thousand hours of work at no cost to local residents. Other unions in Michigan worked with the American Red Cross to deliver bottled water. The work of the Flint Rising Coalition has been crucial in terms of grassroots coordination. Of these efforts to help people in need, Ben Ranger, the Michigan Pipe Trades Association's executive director, said, "This should be all hands on deck. This is our state." As Ed Schroeder, financial secretary of UAW Local 3000, said of Flint's residents: "They need a human response, not another failed politician to offer a handful of nothing."

Of course, it's not just the people of Flint who are offered a handful of nothing. People all over this country pay the price for our overreliance on fossil fuels and disregard for public health. Kamita Grey, for instance, lives in Brandywine, Maryland, a majority black community that has three power plants nearby and two more that have been approved for development. On top of that, there is a coal-ash dump that makes it so difficult to breathe when the wind blows that she cannot go outside. Blanca Hernandez grew up in Richmond, California, near a Chevron oil refinery and several other polluting facilities. For Blanca, it's normal to hear the sound of an alarm bell ringing through the city, telling people to go inside their homes and close all the doors and windows because the air outside can kill you. Oil leaks and gas explosions are also common.

The truth is, if you're black or brown or poor in the United States, you're more likely to be in this kind of situation. Sixty-eight percent of African Americans in the United States live within thirty miles of a coal-fired power plant, and 80 percent of Latinos live in areas that don't meet the Environmental Protection Agency's standards for air quality.

In April 2016, three Lakota Sioux teenagers convened on the north end of the Standing Rock Sioux Reservation (just off the Dakota Access route) to establish a small prayer camp in protest of the Dakota Access Pipeline, part of the Keystone XL Pipeline that would start from Canada and bisect from North Dakota down through Texas. It would move half a million barrels of oil a day underneath the Missouri River, from which the Standing Rock Sioux source their drinking water. Over six months, the prayer group grew from a group of teens and their elders to a nationwide resistance encampment, where everyone from American Indian groups to conservative farmers united in protest. Pipeline backers promised it would create thousands of jobs, but these jobs would only last through the phase of more than one thousand miles of construction—after which the pipeline would yield only about thirty-five permanent jobs. Not only is this an economic red her-

ring, but the pipeline would also move some of the most dangerous, carbon-intensive, and dirtiest oil in the world—called tar-sand
crude. Tar-sand crude had already leaked into the Missouri River,
and that eighty-four gallons' worth of oil was considered small,
routine, and negligible by DAPL employees. That negligible judgment affects the drinking water of millions of people who rely on
the Missouri River—including the Sioux and other towns and
counties dependent on the river's resources.

On December 4, 2016, President Obama's U.S. Army Corps of
Engineers halted the pipeline, as it had done earlier in the face of
protests over the Keystone Pipeline. Sadly, four days into his presidency, Donald Trump signed an executive order to begin clearing
the way for both DAPL and the Keystone XL Pipeline. The entire
Keystone Pipeline operation will create fewer than fifty permanent jobs, despite the millions who would be in harm's way in the
event of a serious leak.

Shoving leaky pipelines down indigenous people's throats is
not a smart or honest way to do economic development. There are
more than one million Native Americans living on reservations in
the United States, and around 14 percent of these families have
no access to electricity. That figure is ten times more than the rest
of the nation. What if we came together with the tribes to fix this?
South Dakota is one of the nation's windiest states, already getting
25 percent of its power from wind. Imagine the jobs and opportunities that Native American–owned wind and solar farms could
create.

Of course it would be wonderful if we were able to fix all
of these environmental problems and create new jobs and economic opportunities in the process. But that would cost billions
of dollars—if not more. Where can we find the cash to fund and
finance the cleaning up and greening up of an entire country?

One woman has a powerful idea that is already making a tremendous difference in California—and could do the same across

America. Her name is Vien Truong, the director of Green For All and the CEO of the Dream Corps. She and her network of advocates have already implemented policy ideas that took a billion dollars from polluters and invested that money to uplift the poorest and most polluted communities in the state.

Vien is a young woman with a remarkable story, one that has made her the ideal champion for using clean-energy solutions to help ordinary people earn a living and save money. Vien is the youngest of eleven children. In the 1970s, her family escaped war-ravaged Vietnam by boat, and Vien was born in a refugee camp. When the Truong family eventually landed in the United States, they settled in Oregon and became migrant farm workers, picking strawberries and snow peas. They later moved down to Oakland, California, where the only jobs available to Vien's parents and older siblings were in manufacturing sweatshops. Vien was the first person in her family to attend college. For her, the definition of success wasn't simply to escape poverty but to figure out how to eradicate it.

In 2012, Vien (then working with the Greenlining Institute) co-led a coalition with the Asian Pacific Environmental Network, Coalition for Clean Air, NAACP, and Natural Resources Defense Council. They wound up making history and moving billions of dollars to address green-energy solutions. Due to their advocacy, the state of California set up an "equitable carbon pricing" program, where the big polluters were being held accountable: Either these companies had to radically reduce the amount of pollution they were pumping into the air, and do it fast, or else they were subject to large fines. In other words, they had to clean up or pay up.

California's carbon-pricing program has led to three billion dollars to fight pollution in "California Climate Investments." These funds have paid for things like transit programs, waste programs, dairy-digester research and development, biofuels, state water projects, affordable housing, and much more.

Vien's coalition partners endorsed and helped to pass a law to ensure that at least 25 percent of the funds from California's carbon-pricing program goes directly to the state's most vulnerable communities, places with the highest levels of poverty and pollution. The fund has already created more than 900 million dollars in investments to these communities, for things like solar panels, energy-efficient improvements, affordable-housing developments, trees for concrete jungles, composting programs, and more.

These dollars are making a positive difference in real people's lives. Vien shared a story with me about Maria Zavala, a woman in Fresno, the city that ranks number one in pollution for the state of California. Thanks to the state's carbon-pricing program, Maria was able to receive free solar panels. She saw her monthly energy bill go down from two hundred dollars to $1.50, because she no longer had to crank up the heat in the winter and the AC in the brutal California summers.

Vien's problem-solving and advocacy led to the Transformative Climate Communities Program, which leverages 140 million dollars from the carbon-pricing program with private capital (in partnership with financial institutions, foundations, public agencies, and other groups) to transform whole communities at a time.

As Vien's example shows, one of the best ways we can open the doors of economic opportunity is to connect our economic vision to our environmental agenda. This means we have to develop practical solutions that help combat pollution and poverty at the same time. People want to breathe clean air and work good jobs; we really can have both.

When it comes to creating jobs, we know that clean energy works. In 2016, the number of jobs in solar grew 25 percent from the year prior, according to figures from the nonprofit Solar Foundation, while jobs in the rest of the economy had less than 2 percent growth. There are almost three million people working in the wind and solar industries alone. Renewable energy companies now create jobs twelve times faster than the rest of the economy. This is a fact we cannot ignore. Our future depends upon finding solutions to heal the land that will work for coal country and the rest of struggling America.

IRONICALLY, IT IS AT THE margins of society that one discovers the moral center. And that is where we must begin to rebuild a politics of possibility. I am not suggesting that we seek a watered-down political centrism. There is nothing in the middle of the road these days but a yellow stripe and dead possums. In fact, the quest for political "moderation" gave us the terrible policies of the 1990s and early 2000s, which just blew up in our faces.

I am interested in the moral center, not the political center. I am searching for common ground, not the "middle ground." I know that common ground can be discovered in surprising places—like in a prison cell, or at a detox center, or on a march with coal miners.

We must go where the pain and peril are greatest and the quest for real solutions is the most desperate. That is where we will be humbled by the limitations of our slogans and our certainties. That is where we will learn to respect the gifts of those with different backgrounds and polar-opposite worldviews—the people with whom we might otherwise and ordinarily disagree but without whom we can't solve the real problems.

Many babies have fallen down many wells. Over the din of the political shouting matches, we all hear their cries. Enough. Let's go rescue them. All of them. In red states and in blue states. And in so doing, we will generate the capacity to rescue each other, ourselves, and our country.

RECLAIMING OUR FOUNDING DREAM

FROM THE VERY BEGINNING OF THIS COUNTRY, AMERICA HAS been two things, not one. We have our founding reality and our founding dream. And the two are not the same.

Our founding reality was ugly and unequal. Nobody can deny that. Take it from Thomas Jefferson himself. If you go to Washington, D.C., you can visit the great Jefferson Memorial. It's this beautiful place, this amazing place. You can climb those grand steps and see for yourself these words from Jefferson, a slave owner, written in marble and stone: "Indeed I tremble for my country when I reflect that God is just, that his justice cannot sleep forever."

You might be thinking, "This doesn't sound like proud triumphalism from the founders." Well, you're right. It doesn't sound like somebody who thinks he's solved all the problems of the world. It sounds like something is off. Jefferson's words reflect a concern that something profound is wrong with the republic, at the very point of its founding.

He's talking about slavery. The violent enslavement and subjugation of hundreds of thousands of human beings of African descent. And he is worried because the founders failed to abolish that monstrous institution; he himself was guilty of the same personally.

There were many more flaws in this country that should have left the founders trembling. At that time a woman could not vote in America. Native American land and lives were being stolen at mind-boggling rates. LGBTQ folks didn't even have a name. Unless you were a straight, white, wealthy landowner, you essentially had no citizenship rights. That was the founding reality: ugly and unequal.

Now, if that's all America ever was, it would command zero allegiance from anyone. It would be impossible for a decent human being to be a patriot. If America were only about keeping that same small circle on top, it would never have stirred the imagination of billions of people over the centuries. In fact, it would never have survived.

But that's not all America was, even at the start. And that's not all we are now.

While you're standing in that same Jefferson Memorial, if you turn your head just a few degrees, you'll see something else. Something astonishing in its beauty. You'll see that the same slaveholding Thomas Jefferson also made this statement: "We hold these truths to be self-evident, that all . . . are created equal."

And there you have our most powerful articulation of the founding dream, which is a beautiful vision about equality.

Our founding reality—that ugly one based in racism, genocide, and slavery—exists today. It lives on in Trump's rhetoric, when he elevates some groups and puts down others, but it sure wasn't born there. Trump's "back in the old days" brand of patriotism—and the dirty right's jingoism and white nationalism– force us back to basics. What is the American project? What are we about? What is patriotism in the age of Donald Trump—and who gets to define the term?

For that matter, who are Americans, anyway? What makes us Americans? Hardly any of us look the same, after all. At the quickest of glances, anyone can distinguish a member of the Chinese Olympic team from a member of the Kenyan Olympic team. But the U.S. Olympic team looks like a global hodgepodge—a walking pack of Skittles. What makes everyone in that group an American? Seriously. Who the heck are we, anyway?

The answer to that question is one that has inspired the world. We are that rainbow-hued people, unique on this earth, who contain in our multitudes every color, every faith, every gender expression and sexuality—every kind of human ever born. And we are living together, in one house, under one law. And we mostly get along. Just a few decades ago, what we do every single day was considered impossible. But here we are—a miracle in human history.

At our best, our mission is simple. For more than two centuries, we have been working to close the gap between the ugliness of our founding reality and the beauty of our founding dream. Each generation tries to narrow that gap a little bit more than the last one did.

No, we will never have a perfect union. But we can always have a *more* perfect union, decade after decade, generation after generation, century after century.

That's who we are. That's what we do. That's what makes us Americans.

America is a good idea brought to life and made real. We exist as an ongoing act of collective will, rooted in the conviction that shared beliefs matter more than shared bloodlines. With all of our flaws, even with our cruel history and current challenges, America is still an idea worth defending—and preserving.

But how? The whole thing seems to be coming apart at the seams.

And it will continue to—as long as we keep listening to the

people at the top. Our national leaders too often model a way of being that I call "all projection, no reflection." As I said earlier, it's all accusation, no confession. Each blames "the other side" for every problem and rarely looks within to find their own opportunities for growth. I sometimes feel like the child of divorcing parents—watching two otherwise decent adults talking past each other and screaming insults, with the whole family's future on the line.

I am sick of the bickering. I bet you are, too.

I would rather listen to people like my dad. Honed by a hardscrabble life in the segregated South, he used the best of both conservative values and liberal principles to get himself out of poverty. For example, he joined the military, educated himself, worked hard, took care of his family. But without an NAACP lawsuit, he might never have become a middle school principal. He badgered local businesses to make charitable donations; he fought local officials to get more funds for disadvantaged schools. Down at city hall, he could sound like a bleeding-heart liberal. But the moment he hit the schoolhouse door, he set aside all the tearjerkers and the hard-luck tales. He never taught his students to pity themselves, and he never taught them to blame the system. Inside that school building, he had one hardheaded, conservative solution for low-income students: Outwork the rich kids. And many of them did.

Sometimes my dad was more conservative than Ronald Reagan and sometimes more liberal than Teddy Kennedy. He had to be. The notion that one set of ideas—let alone one set of elite politicians—could be trusted to serve his interests flew in the face of his lived experience. I remember one conversation we had while watching a televised debate on welfare that characterizes his ideological mash-up beautifully. At one point, he took a big swig from his beer and heaved a weary sigh.

"None of these high-and-mighty people even know what they're talking about," Daddy told me. "None of 'em ever been poor. I grew up poor. I know what it's about. And I'll tell you this: Nothing you just give a poor man as a handout will ever stop him from being poor."

Maybe I was born with a liberal's bleeding heart, but even as a youngster, views like that struck me as being mean-spirited. I pushed back.

"What about giving them money, Daddy? Money would stop them from being poor."

My father shook his head. "Not if you just hand it out." He raised himself up in his recliner and leaned forward. "That might stop 'em from being broke—for maybe a day or two. But if a person is still poor in their skills, poor in their education, poor in their self-esteem, and you hand them a bunch of money? They'll be broke again by tomorrow."

Even if his comment made some basic sense, it still didn't sit right with me. "Then what are people supposed to do? Turn down help and pray for a miracle?"

"Look, son," he said. "Every poor kid has got to climb that ladder out of poverty—on his or her own efforts. That's the responsibility of every poor child. You have to develop yourself so that nobody can keep you poor or make you poor again. You have to make it so you know too much; you bring too many skills to the table. Then you can reach down for the next man and help him climb a rung. But no one can do the real climbing but you."

His voice was quieter when he spoke again.

"That said, grown folks have responsibilities, too."

"Like what?" I asked.

"To make sure that every child in poverty has a ladder to climb," Daddy said, sitting back. "That's what these damn Republicans don't get. They want to cut every program that poor kids need. The brightest child in the world can't climb out of poverty on a ladder that has no rungs on it."

My sister, Angela, has become the kind of person my father

most admired—someone who climbs up one rung of the ladder and then reaches back to help the next person rise. In high school, she started drinking and doing drugs. And it took her—a top student with a megawatt future—off her path. Her journey of recovery from addiction has been challenging; every day has its struggles. But she has been sober since 1995, and today she is a social worker in our hometown. She helps other addicts and at-risk youth who have sustained trauma. She does beautiful work. She has a heart-and-soul commitment to leave behind nobody who needs help.

Away from cable news, Twitter, and election cycles, this is how real life works. We need people and ideas all along the political spectrum. This is how families work. This is how neighborhoods work. And this is how America is supposed to work.

We can find our way back to a better approximation of that ideal. We just need to remember that—at their best—both the liberal and conservative traditions in our country are honorable, vital, and necessary.

For example, conservatives—at their best—stand for *liberty*. They believe in clean, limited government and individual rights. They ask important questions like, "How much does this cost and who's going to pay for it?" Conservatives ask, "Should the government even be providing such-and-such a thing? Why can't a parent or a community group or a religious organization or the free market take care of this?" These are important questions—which liberals sometimes forget to ask.

On the other hand, liberals—at our best—stand for *justice*. We ask a different set of important questions. We say, "Okay, great, we are all for markets, but can America be a great nation if we only do stuff that corporations can make money off?" The answer is, probably not. Then liberals ask, "What about big groups that might run over little groups? What about strong groups that may take advantage of weak groups? Shouldn't we be concerned about that?" Then we ask, "Therefore, shouldn't America's government ensure that there are programs and protections in place, to handle vital social functions that don't make anyone a profit?" These are also good, essential questions.

One side is committed to liberty. The other side is committed to justice. Our schoolchildren get it right every morning; they pledge allegiance to a nation offering *liberty and justice for all.*

These two principles work well together. And when you separate them, there is hell to pay. In the twentieth century, we learned this lesson the hard way. When a government cares only about redistributing wealth but cares nothing about individual liberty, you get totalitarianism. You get government domination over people in the name of social justice, which ends up being simply a different form of injustice. For examples, one needs to look no further than Stalinism in the Soviet Union or North Korea right now. On the other hand, if a government cares only about individual liberty but doesn't give a damn about justice, you get a different kind of tyranny—corporate domination. The big multinational corporations take over everything. They buy your media, they buy your government, and they undermine democracy. Then they poison your water, pollute your air, exploit your workers, and sell you dangerous products. There are countries like that all around the world.

In other words: Liberty without justice is a nightmare. Justice without liberty is a different kind of nightmare. I say this as a dedicated Democrat who wants to see my party run the government. But I want to push the Republicans into opposition, not into oblivion. I would never want conservative proposals or proponents to disappear from the public square. I value too highly the right's best critiques, insights, and traditions.

No bird can fly with only a left wing. No bird can fly with only a right wing. Both sides still need each other. Our creed is *E pluribus unum,* which means "out of many, one." The liberals want to see more respect for diversity (the *pluribus*), and the conservatives desire an un-hyphenated American identity (the *unum*)—but both sets of values are present in the same national motto. That's the genius of America.

Mutual respect, even in passionate disagreement, must be the goal. Too many liberals look at the red states the same way that colonizers once viewed developing countries. All they see is a bunch of backward, unwashed, uneducated heathens who need to be converted to the NPR religion and force-fed kale until they see the light. That kind of disdain reveals itself in thousands of different ways. But you can't lead people you don't love. You can't rally people you don't respect. Throughout history, people have resisted being conquered or converted by contemptuous outsiders. If we continue to show up with that attitude, our every word and gesture just fertilizes the soil for white nationalists and others who traffic in the politics of resentment. Without knowing it, we give ammo to the very forces decent-minded people want to defeat.

That said, too many conservatives act as if they are the only "real Americans," who somehow "own" the very idea of patriotism. They should not allow themselves to be seduced into a smug jingoism, built on put-downs and slogans without substance. It's too easy to sing "America the Beautiful" and not hear a single word of the song. That's cheap patriotism. Some of us go out and defend America's beauty from the clear-cutters and the oil-spillers. That's deep patriotism. It's really easy to take selfies at the Statue of Liberty. That's cheap patriotism. Some of us know that Lady Liberty is our Mother of Exiles, as engraved in the poem at the base of the statue. So we go fight for the rights and dignity of immigrants. That's deep patriotism. It's easy to say the Pledge of Allegiance but never act on the values it invokes. That's cheap patriotism. Some of us try to make real the idea of liberty and justice for everyone—by defending the folks in prisons and deportation centers, sticking up for folks who are terrified in mosques, standing with people who are fearful in synagogues. That's deep patriotism.

So this is a game that two can play. If you don't want anyone to challenge your patriotism, then please stop challenging ours.

What should bring us back together is the idea of American exceptionalism. Because America is truly an exceptional place. The Iroquois Federation's template helped to make our nation exceptional. The anti-colonial rebels who wrote the Constitution made us exceptional. The abolitionists and the suffragettes who deepened democracy made us exceptional. So did Rachel Carson and Teddy Roosevelt, Fannie Lou Hamer and Dr. Martin Luther King, Dolores Huerta and Cesar Chavez, Audre Lorde and Larry Kramer. Americans of every color, gender, and creed have made our nation extraordinary. And now it is our turn.

Breakdowns like the one we are going through now are unavoidable. After all, the American experiment flies in the face of ten thousand years of human history. For most of that time, it was perfectly acceptable to chop another person up into small parts just because he or she hailed from a different tribe. We now demand better of the world. And as Americans, we expect better of one another. But let us not underestimate the heroism of our cause. We are asking a lot of our neighbors and ourselves.

America is hard to do. And sometimes people get scared. They may say the wrong thing. They may vote out of anger or fear, on any side. They may even give up on the country itself and seek refuge in some smaller subgroup or sect. I know because I have done all those things myself at one time or another. We need to acknowledge that we are trying to do something hard here in America.

And, as with all hard things, there comes a time when we must redouble our efforts to listen to one another and make progress. This is the real America. It's messy. But it works.

TRUMP WILL NEVER BE IMPEACHED—SO VOTE!

T HIS BOOK WAS FIRST PUBLISHED IN OCTOBER OF 2017, roughly a year after Donald Trump was elected the forty-fifth President of the United States. I wrote it in the wake of that monumental upset, when the world of American politics had been turned completely upside down. I tried to reckon with how we got to a place where the bipartisan political establishment was so odious to so many people that Donald Trump's bullying and lying could help him (or at least not hurt him) to prevail at the polls.

As these pages show, I worried then that Trump would further divide American society and further marginalize already vulnerable groups. Since then, my concerns have been vindicated as the political divide has only grown wider—and Trump has continued to target immigrants, transgendered people, and others.

With this book, I also chose to advance several "common ground" solutions that could open a door to bipartisan progress on important issues. But even in those areas, the Trump administration has largely done damage. Consider the categories of his destructive efforts:

ENVIRONMENTAL CRIMES

The Trump Administration targeted at least sixty environmental programs for delay or rollback in 2017, putting all of our climate and clean-energy progress at risk. His moves included withdrawing the U.S. from the Paris Climate Agreement, attempting to roll back the Clean Power Plan, weakening clean car standards, and proposing to slash the U.S. EPA budget by 31 percent.

The administration has made eliminating federal regulations a priority, targeting environmental rules and Obama-era policies meant to fight climate change, all to relieve burdens on the fossil fuel industry. In the name of trying to go after job-killing regulation, this administration is increasing the amount of pollution and poison in our air and water, implementing child-killing deregulation. This means more asthma for kids, more cancer for kids.

In March 2017, the Environmental Protection Agency's director, Scott Pruitt, announced he would refuse to ban the pesticide chlorpyrifos from being sprayed on food, despite findings that even trace amounts of chlorpyrifos can interfere with children's brain development. The EPA also weakened the rules that limit the amount of pollution cars and trucks can emit. These actions represent serious crimes against both the public trust and public health. And this is only the latest in a series of moves by the administration to roll back protections for cleaner air. Especially for low-income communities and communities of color, decisions like this can result in illness and even death.

CRIMINAL JUSTICE ROLLBACKS

Donald Trump's campaign rhetoric, election, and early actions alarmed many criminal justice reformers. Most damaging was his appointment of Jeff Sessions as attorney general.

Within the first months of Donald Trump's presidency, his ad-

ministration proudly undid much of the progress made during
President Barack Obama's tenure. Trump doubled down on the
use of private prisons, rolled back consent decrees and oversight of
some of America's most troubled police departments, and promised to seek the harshest punishments even in the case of low-level
drug crimes.

Attorney General Jeff Sessions rescinded an Obama-era memo
to judges discouraging them from incarcerating people for not
being able to pay fines and fees. He announced a new crackdown
on marijuana. He also issued a memo forcing federal prosecutors
to pursue the harshest penalties and stiffest prison sentences in
criminal cases. Because of these actions, the federal prison population was predicted to increase in 2018, after a period of steep
decline under the Obama administration. Unfortunately, we know
communities of color will be disproportionately harmed.

Partially as a result, the nationwide momentum to fix our justice system has begun to stall, even at the state and local levels.
We have already begun to see some efforts to roll back recent
criminal justice victories in Louisiana, Alaska, and even California. Advocates have soldiered on, but hope has been fading.

The one bright spot is the FIRST STEP Act, a prison reform
initiative championed by U.S. representative Hakeem Jeffries (D-
NY) and U.S. representative Doug Collins (R-GA). West Wing
advisor (and Trump son-in-law) Jared Kushner gave the legislation
his full backing and I got personally involved as well, even appear-
ing with Jared at the White House to raise awareness for it. Kushner's own father served time in a federal prison, so he has a special
interest in criminal justice issues. Jessica Jackson and her #cut50
team (see page 143) also worked tirelessly to champion the bill.
Some liberals opposed our efforts, but we decided that the progress for prisoners was worth it. The bill passed the House in late
May 2018 in a landslide victory: 355-58. If signed into law, the bill
will nudge the federal prison system away from a punishment-

based model and toward a more rehabilitative one. That said, this modest proposal is a far cry from the comprehensive criminal justice reform that members of Congress were debating and preparing to pass under President Obama.

JUDICIAL APPOINTMENTS

Trump has set a record with the number of judicial appointments he made in his first year. In addition to appointing Neil Gorsuch to the Supreme Court, Trump has (as of this writing) appointed nearly forty federal judges (lifelong positions), including at least twenty to the appeals court—more than any previous first-year president.

According to Pew Research, his record-high appointment rates have also been met by record high dissent. With each confirmation receiving an average of twenty-three "no" votes from the U.S. Senate floor, this level of Senate opposition is by far the highest for any president's judicial appointments since the Senate expansion in 1959. Trump has made it his habit to appoint extreme ideologues, many of whom have failed to meet the minimal standards of the American Bar Association.

In sum, the forty-fifth president is moving the nation in the wrong direction. And by stacking the courts with unqualified ideologues, Trump is making it harder for future leaders to undo the damage he is causing. Defeating Trump and Trumpism is an even more urgent task now than it was in 2016.

I also wrote this book in the hope that readers of all political stripes might be motivated to try to build bridges with one another, regardless of what Trump says, does, or doesn't do. I wanted to help quiet the rancor and focus the conversation on solutions— like criminal justice reform, responding to the addiction crisis, and creating jobs for tomorrow in clean tech and high tech. That's been my life's work, and I continue to try to have meaningful dialogue with people of all backgrounds. I am happy to report that since publication, I've heard from many readers that my work has, indeed, sparked conversation and led to some better understanding. That's the good news.

Unfortunately, there is also very bad news.

Ex–FBI director Robert Mueller continues his methodical investigation into possible Russian meddling in our electoral system and collusion between Trump's team and the Russians. In so many ways, Donald Trump has created a serious danger for the most important center of power in the world.

But the real danger is not necessarily the most obvious threat. And it does not imperil the power center you might assume.

The biggest danger Mueller's investigation poses is actually to *the anti-Trump resistance itself,* by distracting the #resistance from the hard work of voting Trump and his forces out of office. The constellation of forces who oppose Trump are a potentially formidable force, capable of rescuing our republic. But by creating the false hope that Trump will be leaving the White House in handcuffs—any day now—"Mueller mania" continues to distract Americans from the hard work of building a pro-democracy movement that could actually defeat Trumpism.

Too many progressives treat Robert Mueller like the tooth fairy. They expect to wake up one morning, switch on NPR, and learn that Mueller has left a functioning democracy for us under our pillows. That is not going to happen.

FALLACY OR FANTASY: LIBERALS FAIL TO GRASP REALITY

Ever since Trump came down the escalator in 2015 to announce his candidacy, too many liberals have been comforting themselves with one version or another of the same fallacious argument: "Trump will—at some point—self-destruct."

Within the anti-Trump movement, this sentiment has risen to the level of a religious conviction. Blinded by this article of faith, passionate anti-Trumpers told us the brash billionaire would never win the Republican nomination, because his unforgivable gaffes would ruin him—eventually. We know now that they were very, very wrong. After Trump captured the nomination and took over the GOP, the reality TV star's critics were certain he would never be elected president, because he had offended too many women and people of color. Wrong again. After he won the November 2016 election, some liberals even comforted themselves by suggesting that the Electoral College would simply refuse to seat him. Again, no.

Now the same crowd rocks itself to sleep, whispering another version of the same vain hope: "Trump will be impeached soon and then removed from office."

Let me be clear: This idea is ridiculous.

Consider this: The U.S. House of Representatives has successfully impeached only two presidents—in nearly 250 years. And the U.S. Senate has removed a grand total of zero. NONE.

Most importantly, please keep in mind: No political party has ever impeached one of its own members—ever. For example, in 1868, Andrew Johnson was impeached by his political enemies, not by members of his own party. In 1998, it was a Republican-controlled Congress that impeached Democrat Bill Clinton, over the strenuous objections of Clinton's fellow party members. For nearly a quarter of a millennium, when it comes to impeachment, party loyalty has overridden every other loyalty, every time. No president has ever had a Congress controlled by his own party even consider impeaching him.

In light of those facts, there is no reason to think that anything will be different this time around. In fact, far from it: Trump's own

Republican Party controls the U.S. House of Representatives today. That is the very body where articles of impeachment must originate. The modern GOP is more conservative and hyper-partisan than its previous incarnations—by almost every measure. So it is ludicrous to believe that today's House Republicans would suddenly discover historic and unprecedented levels of high-minded moral clarity and vote to remove one of their own from the Oval Office. As long as the GOP controls that chamber, it is a safe bet that impeachment proceedings will never take place—no matter how much Trump's antics erode democratic norms or offend liberal sensibilities.

THE U.S. SENATE WILL NEVER REMOVE TRUMP

But suppose the Democrats take the U.S. House (likely) and U.S. Senate (unlikely, but possible) in 2018. Then might Trump's fate be sealed?

Nope. Because the U.S. Senate has never removed a sitting president, even after the U.S. House had impeached him. Not once. It bears noting that majorities in the U.S. House impeached both Johnson and Clinton, but the U.S. Senate failed to convict and remove them—so both men finished their full terms.

A Democrat-controlled U.S. House could decide to impeach Trump once a week; it would not matter. It would still take two-thirds of the senators to subsequently convict an impeached president and thereby throw Trump out of office. Two-thirds! We rarely have two-thirds of U.S. senators who can agree on anything at all; I am not sure they would all vote to agree that all of them are senators.

So it is insane to believe that, within this hopelessly divided upper chamber, a supermajority would unite to evict Trump. After all, such a large percentage would have to include Republican senators from red states where Trump remains very popular, no matter what he does. If those senators helped to vote Trump out of office, they would be voting themselves out of office, too—because Trump's fans back home would recruit pro-Trump candidates to run against those "traitors" in the next primary elections. Few red state senators would be willing to commit political suicide by siding with Democrats against their own party's president.

TRUMP WILL NEVER QUIT

The final fantasy that gives hope to the more naïve wing of the anti-Trump movement is the notion that Trump is so miserable, harassed, and overwhelmed in the Oval Office that he will simply resign and slink away. For this idea, there is at least a precedent. The disgraced Richard Nixon was neither impeached nor removed; he saw the tables turning against him and simply quit.

But Trump is never going to do that.

Trump's galaxy-sized ego loves being the center of attention. Those who think he is unhappy in office take his whining on social media too seriously. As president, his every utterance and tweet is instantly global news. Everything he does and says is obsessed over by millions of people, not just across the country but around the world. Why would a world-class narcissist give all of that up, just so he could sit at home and watch President Pence on his television every day?

It is also worth noting that his businesses continue to thrive around the world; the Trump brand is bigger than ever. Being president is not costing him financially. Plus he has children— Don Jr. and Ivanka are the likeliest candidates—who could run for office themselves someday and turn the Trump business empire into a formidable political dynasty. Donald Trump will never voluntarily give up his role as the star of the biggest reality-television show in history.

And there is one more reason why The Donald would never

leave the Oval Office of his own volition: As president, he can pardon anyone of any federal crime. He holds the ultimate "trump" card: instant exoneration of anyone he cares to defend, close associates and family members very much included. (Trump even believes that he can pardon himself, and it might take the U.S. Supreme Court a year or more to determine whether he has that power.)

To review: The U.S. House won't impeach Trump. Even if the U.S. House did impeach him, the U.S. Senate will never muster enough votes to remove him. Unlike Nixon, Trump won't ever quit voluntarily. All of these facts and factors point to one inescapable reality: As a practical matter, there is zero chance that Congress or law enforcement will remove Trump from office before the 2020 election.

So what should those who oppose Trump do?

THE PARKLAND KIDS ARE RIGHT: "VOTE THEM OUT!"

Freed from the fallacy or fantasy of "impeachment" as a viable solution, we can turn our attention back to the real business of making a democracy work: *winning elections.*

After all, Trump won not just because he inflamed racial divisions and exploited a populist wave. He won because Hillary Clinton's supporters refused to believe that Trump could win, took her victory for granted, and didn't work passionately or intelligently enough to ensure her victory. Obama's back-to-back triumphs created a false sense of security among Democrats—and bred a lethal form of complacency. Democrats forgot how hard they had been forced to work in 2008. Back then, supporters fanned out across the country to elect Obama. They volunteered in swing states. They held fundraisers in their living rooms. They used their own cell phones to create people-powered phone banks, contacting potential voters in critical areas and begging them to vote.

They worked their butts off to make sure Obama won. They repeated their efforts in 2012—and they were rewarded both times.

And yet, during those same eight years, the Republicans were getting skilled at winning elections, too. In fact, they won practically every time and every place that Obama wasn't on the ballot. For example, the GOP took the U.S. House in 2010 and the U.S. Senate in 2014—the two national, Obama-era elections that didn't feature Obama's name as an option in any race. Additionally, during the Obama years, the Democrats lost several governorships and more than 1,000 formerly blue seats at the state level. The pattern was clear: Without Obama's unique magic, Democrats struggled to win elections. Heading into the 2016 election, there was very little to suggest that the "Obama Coalition" could beat anyone—without one man's personal magnetism directly holding it together. Far from being smug and overconfident, every Democrat should have been very, very worried about Hillary Clinton's chances.

If these repeated thrashings at the ballot box failed to teach Democrats a lesson, then certainly the catastrophe of 2016 should have been the final wake-up call. Right now, every progressive in the country should be working hard to register voters, preparing to raise money for the party, and getting ready to travel to key districts to win tough elections in 2018 and beyond.

THE "TRUMP IS HITLER" FALLACY HURTS DEMS

To understand why so few progressives are psychologically and emotionally focused on winning elections, it is important to deconstruct what has become the standard liberal narrative about the forty-fifth president.

This is how many anti-Trump liberals see America's predicament:

- Trump is the main enemy;
- The immediate danger is authoritarianism or even fascism;

- Trump is like Hitler;
- Trump's crimes are like Watergate, which drove Nixon from office;
- Therefore, the solution is: "Impeach Trump now."

This narrative tends to focus the mind on ongoing investigations, not upcoming elections. But what if every step of that argument is wrong?

What if the following five points are closer to the truth?

- Putin is the main enemy;
- The main danger is a crippled America—divided and dysfunctional;
- Trump is more like Silvio Berlusconi—a clown and possibly a kleptocrat, but not a mass murderer;
- Trump's crimes are more like Iran-Contra, a 1980s scandal that sent some major figures to jail but did not end Reagan's presidency;
- Therefore, the real solution is: "Vote them out!"

Trump is not cut in the mold of a murderous dictator like Germany's Hitler or Italy's Mussolini. Instead, Trump is more like a U.S. version of Italy's Berluosconi—a corrupt, crass kleptocrat who degraded and debased his nation's vital institutions. He is dangerous—especially to racial and religious minorities. But he has no plans to cancel elections or set up death camps. We are far from that kind of nightmare scenario.

Therefore, the immediate threat does not take the shape of a diabolical leader forging a strong, fascist state that can impose its will on a terrified populace. The immediate danger is, ironically, the very opposite—not a strong America united to do evil, but a weak America too divided to do good (even the good that desperately needs doing). Our nation is in danger of spiraling down into a divided, dysfunctional society—one incapable of accomplishing anything except occasionally passing out some tax breaks. This is especially tragic, given the big challenges—from climate disruption to technology wiping out tens of millions of jobs—that demand big solutions and bold action.

Who has the most to gain from this kind of division? Not our internal partisan opponents, but our external geopolitical enemies. Weakening all democracies—especially the United States—seems to be the main aim of Russia's Vladimir Putin. And I fear that both sides of our political divide are at times helping him achieve his goals. If Putin is the real enemy, then our challenge shifts. We have a duty to avoid unnecessarily inflaming divisions—even as we work to thwart Trump.

Some crimes may ultimately be attributed to the Trump campaign and administration, but without incontrovertible proof, Trump will likely escape unscathed. It is useful to remember that the Reagan administration got caught unlawfully selling arms to Iran and using the proceeds to illegally fund right-wing rebels in Nicaragua. Plenty of stooges and fall guys went to prison over the Iran-Contra flap. But the Gipper himself remained untouched. Then his vice president, George H. W. Bush, proceeded to win the next national election in 1988. A massive scandal that involved illegal coordination with a foreign power and actual law breaking did not even ding the Reagan-Bush administration—even though Democrats controlled the U.S. Congress at that time. The idea that a similar scandal would somehow terminate the Trump presidency is far-fetched, if not absurd.

Taken all together, the more sober analysis reinforces the wisdom of the young students who survived the massacre at Parkland High School. Rejecting the standard "thoughts and prayers" slogan that takes over social media after every mass shooting, the youngsters advanced a new rallying cry: "Vote them out." What I propose is equally simple: We should use the next

American election to address the negative results of the previous American election.

2018: THE MOST IMPORTANT MIDTERM ELECTIONS EVER

All of this means that anti-Trump forces need to get busy. Whether you are a Democrat or a Republican, a progressive or a conservative, you should hope that Democrats gain seats during the 2018 midterm elections. On the right, sensible Republicans will never recover their standing within their own party—not until American voters deliver a devastating, catastrophic rebuke to Trumpism at the ballot box.

On the left, Democrats should seek a massive victory, because the very attempt will force the party to evolve beyond its anti-Trump outrage. They will have to start to appeal to a broader constituency. Heartland Democrats in purple districts (and the coastal donors that must support them) will have to engage millions of independent voters. These Americans don't care about Trump's tweets or his porn star mistresses. Therefore, progressive candidates will have to focus more on their proposals and solutions for job creation, healthcare, and education. That development itself will be healthy.

If the Democrats do take back the U.S. House in the midterm elections, the dynamic will begin to shift. The power of the purse strings will be in the hands of those who oppose the Trump agenda. And dozens of powerful committee chairs will be able to convene hearings and issue subpoenas to explore and challenge any number of irregularities.

But it won't be easy. To be clear: Just to restore any semblance of representative democracy, the Democrats will need to overshoot the runway and win in a landslide. As I pointed out earlier in this book, we now have one-party minority rule in the nation's capital.

More Americans voted for Hillary Clinton than Trump, but the Electoral College nullified that result. If you add up the national totals for the 2016 Congressional races, more than one million more Americans voted for Democrats than voted for Republicans running for seats in the U.S. House. But GOP gerrymandering at the state level has ensured that Republicans have an unnatural advantage. Therefore, the Republicans got the majority of seats in the U.S. House, even though they won a minority of the total votes in the country. Reversing this reality will require massive effort.

A broad, smart political movement could curtail the Trump administration's reign of error. And yet the belief that Trump will be impeached creates a dangerous distraction from the work of building such a movement. Trump is a cad, a bigot, and an awful president. But Putin's plot to permanently cripple America from within poses the bigger long-term threat.

Properly led, the anti-Trump, pro-democracy movement could be Putin's worst nightmare—and America's best hope.

BRIDGE-BUILDING RESOURCES

Many people find themselves asking: What can I do now? How can I make a positive difference for the world, for my family? How do I learn and grow?

The following suggestions are meant to help. They do not represent a complete response—neither comprehensive nor cleanly categorized (since some of the sources listed don't fit neatly into any bracket). But I do offer a starting point. To move forward, Americans don't all have to agree—but we do need to better understand one another. We need to recognize the lives, ideas, and frustrations of those who have completely different goals and values. We also have to get active, putting our minds and hearts to use in making America work again.

My hope is that these bridge-building resources will help you gain an understanding of those on the "other side." Minimally, it is always good to "know your enemy." Beyond that, many of us are suffering from a form of intellectual scurvy; we need to consume a broader diet of ideas and perspectives—if nothing else, just to keep our own philosophies fresh and interesting. All of us can learn something valuable from listening to opposing views. In the end, it may turn out that our old ideologies, worldviews, and understandings must be reconsidered and upgraded for the new digital age. If so, engaging a broad range of insights would be good preparation for any of us.

I have also included a section called Diversify Your Feed in both parts of this appendix. One of the easiest ways to start embracing the Messy Truth is to diversify your news feed. Clicking on "follow" is a low-risk way to start building a deeper understanding of what others are thinking. You may find connection and develop compassion—but if not, you will certainly be well-read on your opposition. Below is a list of some of the people I follow—people I agree with, people who interest me, and some people of significant influence whom I wholeheartedly disagree with.

Please visit www.messytruth.com for a broader list. There you can suggest resources you found helpful to add to the directory.

BOOKS, PODCASTS, AND MOVIES TO HELP YOU REACH ACROSS DIVIDES

Creating a reading list was one of the more difficult tasks for this book. I am and always have been a book nerd, and picking a favorite book is like picking a favorite child. If you are like me and enjoy learning the old-fashioned way, this list is a good start. I interspersed a few classics along with modern reads and tried to cover a range of topics.

Following the book list are podcasts, documentaries, and other long-form media; they dig into the critical issues facing our country and offer unique and divergent perspectives.

Ten Books for Understanding Red-State America

1. *Strangers in Their Own Land,* by Arlie Hochschild
This book dives deep into the outlook and anxieties of working-

class whites in red-state America. Hochschild develops a complex view of Tea Party–conservative thinking, which makes this a good book for challenging the progressive tendency to jump to conclusions about why so many conservatives appear to act against what liberal's describe as "their own self-interest."

2. *Hillbilly Elegy: A Memoir of a Family and Culture in Crisis,* **by J. D. Vance**
Vance paints a picture of a family's history in Appalachia, bringing up the values, struggles, and outcomes that define their difficult experience. The kind of sympathy and discomfort that this book brings up can push people on the left to expand their ideas about who can be "oppressed" in this country. A humanizing read.

3. *The Conservative Heart: How to Build a Fairer, Happier, and More Prosperous America,* **by Arthur C. Brooks**
Brooks writes this book as a challenge to those who believe in conservative economic policy to communicate their ideals not just with the head but with the heart. Reading this book allows liberals to consider what conservatism might feel like if the messaging around it moved away from only pragmatism and included more care, concern, and compassion.

4. *White Trash: The 400-Year Untold History of Class in America,* **by Nancy Isenberg**
With this book, Isenberg develops a unique analysis of our nation's legacies of inequality and class struggle, by focusing solely on a segment of our country's disregarded low-income white population. Many from this population supported Trump, so Isenberg's book is valuable for getting a deeper sense of the "why" behind some aspects of Trump's rise.

5. *Who Really Cares: The Surprising Truth About Compassionate Conservatism,* **by Arthur C. Brooks**
This book challenges some classic ideas that people on the left are more compassionate than those on the right. Brooks pushes his reader to move away from the false distinction between the bleeding-heart liberal and the stone-hearted conservative.

6. *The New Minority: White Working Class Politics in an Age of Immigration and Inequality,* **by Justin Gest**
Gest contextualizes the rise of Trump and the radicalization of the right by focusing on the impacts of loss of status and political influence. This is a helpful book for thinking about the effects of political marginalization and economic disenfranchisement.

7. *Listen, Liberal: Or, What Ever Happened to the Party of the People?,* **by Thomas Frank**
This is the perfect book for liberals who are willing to take a long, hard look in the mirror. With a critique of the pervasive disconnection from working-class America and the general elitism that has come to define the Democratic Party, Frank's message is a humbling pill that many on the left would be advised to swallow.

8. *Intellectuals and Race,* **by Thomas Sowell**
This book is Sowell's controversial project to focus on the negative impacts of overgeneralization and selective thought when attempting to make sense of racial disparity. He attempts to pinpoint where particular racial or ethnic groups are harmed rather than helped by intellectual campaigns for justice. Read this book if you want to confront some of the left's logic on social difference and think about how progressive liberal discourse can read as dogma.

9. *Why You're Wrong About the Right: Behind the Myths—The Surprising Truth About Conservatives,* **by S. E. Cupp and Brett Joshpe**

This book challenges liberals to diversify the way they think about political conservatives. As a society, we tend to ascribe both conservatives and liberals with very narrow, unbending characteristics. This book is a good way to work on reconfiguring our ideas of what a conservative has to be like.

10. *Coming Apart: The State of White America, 1960–2010,* **by Charles Murray**

I despise Murray's previous work (especially his 1994 book, *The Bell Curve*), which flirted with eugenics and dressed up white supremacist dogma in intellectual robes. But *Coming Apart* is a useful read for people who tend to be concerned only about disparity between—but not within—races. This book analyzes some of what has been and is contributing to class divides among white people, which impacts the way low-income white people tend to vote in this country.

What to Watch and Listen to for a Better Understanding of Red-State America

1. Documentary Film: *Accidental Courtesy: Daryl Davis, Race & America,* **by Matt Ornstein**

This film follows a middle-aged black man from the South as he befriends members of the KKK. He develops such strong camaraderie with many that some ultimately decide to leave the Klan. This work is an extreme example of the good that can come from reaching out to understand the other side.

2. Documentary Film: *The Armor of Light,* **by Abigail Disney**

This film follows the unlikely partnership between a far-right evangelical minister and a mother whose unarmed son was shot and killed in Florida. Together, they engage members of their pro-gun community in difficult conversation about what it means to be both pro-gun and pro-life. They ponder whether we need a new moral framework for understanding U.S. gun culture. An interesting piece of work on coming together and on holding conflicting beliefs side by side.

3. Photojournalism by Chris Arnade in *The Guardian*: **www.theguardian.com/profile/chris-arnade**

Arnade's images paint a striking, raw picture of what life in red-state America can look like for poor blacks and whites. Taking images of people who are addicted and living in poverty, Arnade's images are worth sitting with. For those who live in different parts of the country or the world, this is a good resource for actually *seeing* the faces of those whom we talk about but rarely talk to.

4. Podcast: *Uncommon Knowledge,* **with Peter Robinson: itunes.apple.com/us/podcast/uncommon -knowledge-audio-edition/id384420950?mt=2**

This podcast dives into social, political, and economic discussions that ask tough questions and do not toe a party line. Refreshing.

5. Podcast: *Waking Up,* **with Sam Harris: www .samharris.org/podcast**

Sam Harris's podcast is full of interesting topics on politics, religion, history, human behavior, and more. He takes an intellectual, curiosity-based approach to each conversation, not confined to a particular political ideology.

DIVERSIFY YOUR FEED: UNDERSTAND RED-STATE AMERICA

Here is a list of writers, educators, performers, pundits, hosts of television and podcast series, and more that I turn to for a variety of takes on the conservative outlook.

- Scott Adams (cartoonist, commentator), @ScottAdamsSays
- Dan Bongino (radio host), @Dbongino
- Tucker Carlson (TV host, author), @tuckercarlson
- Governor Chris Christie (R-NJ), @ChrisChristie
- Senator Susan Collins (R-ME), @SenatorCollins
- Ann Coulter (author, TV personality), @anncoulter
- S. E. Cupp (author and regular political contributor), @secupp
- Governor Nathan Deal (R-GA), @NathanDeal
- Philip DeFranco (YouTube personality, host of The Philip DeFranco Show—PDS), @PhillyD
- Speaker Newt Gingrich, @newtgingrich
- Sean Hannity (author, TV host), @seanhannity
- Laura Ingraham, @ingrahamangle
- Governor John Kasich (R-OH), @JohnKasich
- Rep. Steve King (R-IA), @SteveKingIA
- Rep. Adam Kinzinger (R-IL), @RepKinzinger
- Tomi Lahren, @TomiLahren
- Senator Mike Lee (R-UT), @SenMikeLee
- Mark R. Levin (author, radio host), @marklevinshow
- Dana Loesch, @dloesch
- Frank Luntz (Republican strategist and expert message-developer), @FrankLuntz
- Michelle Malkin (conservative blogger, political commentator, and author), @michellemalkin
- Ana Navarro (Republican strategist and political contributor, originally from Nicaragua), @ananavarro

- Dana Perino (author, political contributor to Fox News, co-host of *The Five,* White House press secretary under George W. Bush), @DanaPerino
- Dave Rubin (comedian, television personality, host of political talk show *The Rubin Report*), @RubinReport
- Speaker Paul Ryan (R-WI), @SpeakerRyan
- Senator Ben Sasse (R-NE), @SenSasse
- Steve Schmidt (Republican campaign strategist), @SteveSchmidtSES
- Arnold Schwarzenegger (former governor of California, actor, advocate, and philanthropist), @Schwarzenegger
- Ben Shapiro (author, political commentator, creator of *The Daily Wire* and the online podcast *The Ben Shapiro Show*), @benshapiro
- Christina Hoff Sommers (author, educator, and host of video blog series *The Factual Feminist*), @CHSommers
- Allen West (radio host, author), @allenwest

Ten Books for Understanding Blue-State America

1. *The New Jim Crow: Mass Incarceration in the Age of Colorblindness,* by Michelle Alexander
This book is an important read for looking critically at the impacts of our country's criminal-justice system on people of color. The marginalizing laws of the twentieth-century Jim Crow era meant to prevent black people from reaching full citizenship may be written out, but Michelle Alexander paints a profound picture of the ways that our criminal-justice system is a massive tool for keeping that same marginalization alive.

2. *Between the World and Me* by Ta-Nehisi Coates
This book is—in one word—powerful. Written in the form of a letter to his fifteen-year-old son, with this book Coates offers us

an opportunity to sit with the big questions and worries that linger (sometimes known, sometimes unconscious) in the minds of black boys and men in the United States. With more media attention than ever before focused on black killings by police in this country, this book is an important opportunity to learn about, think about, and meditate on one black man's eloquent and impassioned appeal to his son to recognize and step into the struggles that will mark his life.

3. *Dog Whistle Politics: How Coded Racial Appeals Have Reinvented Racism and Wrecked the Middle Class,* **by Ian Haney López**
This book is a solid resource for understanding political messaging around poverty, race, and motive. López points to examples like Reagan-era campaigns around the "welfare queen" and shows how such messaging becomes reified and ultimately is used to influence social outlook and sway political opinion.

4. *Hillbilly Nationalists, Urban Race Rebels, and Black Power,* **by Amy Sonnie and James Tracy**
Just as they are today, poor and working-class whites were ignored—and even despised—by progressives in the 1960s. This book introduces you to poor and working-class whites during the civil-rights era who aided the cause of justice, forming history-making alliances to address poverty, racism, and sexism. For bridge-building on the left and forming a more inclusive movement, this is a must-read.

5. *Bad Feminist,* **by Roxane Gay**
This was a difficult decision, since there are so many important books on feminism, but I chose this one because it is an accessible piece for those who want to read about the ways that feminism can look and feel different for different people. Gay takes a very human approach in this book and sends a message that there is no

one right way to "do feminism" and that, like every great movement, feminism is complicated and flawed. Gay argues that it is *with* those flaws and that complexity that feminism has the power to genuinely liberate people.

6. *Redefining Realness: My Path to Womanhood, Identity, Love, & So Much More,* by Janet Mock

Mock offers us a very personal recollection of growing up poor in the United States as a mixed-race person who transitioned from male to female early in life. Though her experience is specific, her writing makes it universally relatable. Anyone who wants to sit with questions about trans identity, or identity in general, social pressure, and seeking personal truth should read this book.

7. *State of the Union: A Century of American Labor,* by Nelson Lichtenstein

This book is a useful primer for understanding the history of the labor movement in this country. Lichtenstein gives a detailed account of the evolution of labor—the struggles, surges, wins, and losses that have taken place since the Progressive Era—and how labor is a critical element for achieving democracy.

8. *Open Veins of Latin America* by Eduardo Galeano

This classic book is a good one to turn to for examining the impacts of colonialism on Latin America by the Western world. Placing Western settlement in the context of economic exploitation and political domination, Galeano's historical work helps to explain the United States' and Europe's responsibility in terms of social and developmental unrest in Latin American regions.

9. *An Indigenous Peoples' History of the United States,* by Roxanne Dunbar-Ortiz

Dunbar-Ortiz tells the story of this country's founding through an indigenous American lens and bases the telling of it on an analysis of U.S. policy. Dunbar-Ortiz aims to show that the United States' founding policy was to exploit, displace, and ultimately eliminate indigenous Americans. Turn to this book for a current and un-blinking look at the intentions and impacts of U.S. colonization of indigenous American lands.

10. *A People's History of the United States,* by Howard Zinn

This book looks at our country's history from the perspective of "the people." It tells a story of conflict and power struggles be-tween the elite class and everyone else, and it is a helpful resource for understanding current-day movements challenging unequal distributions of power and access.

What to Watch and Listen to for a Better Understanding of Blue-State America

1. Documentary Film: *13th,* by Ava DuVernay

Watch *13th* to get a compelling historical take on the criminaliza-tion of black people in the United States. This film is particularly useful for looking at the ways that black people and poor people of color have been locked up and disenfranchised—from the eras of slavery to mass incarceration.

2. Documentary Film: *The Waiting Room,* by Peter Nicks

This film takes us through a day in the life of Oakland's High-land Hospital emergency room. The result is a gut-wrenching depiction of how patients and staff alike do their best to navigate a difficult public-healthcare system. Many uninsured, waiting for hours or days, hope dwindling—this is a powerful film that will make the dire nature of our healthcare landscape utterly ap-parent.

3. Documentary Film: *The Trans List,* interviews by Janet Mock

The Trans List is an HBO documentary featuring interviews with eleven popular transgendered people. The interviews touch on topics like childhood, family, work, love, moments of accomplishment and difficulty, and identity in general. This film allows us to take in a range of trans people's experiences and diversify our ideas about what it is to be trans in the United States.

4. Checklist: "White Privilege: Unpacking the Invisible Knapsack," by Peggy McIntosh: www.deanza.edu/faculty /lewisjulie/White%20Priviledge%20Unpacking%20 the%20Invisible%20Knapsack.pdf

The primary goal of this checklist is to get people thinking about different aspects of their lives that work for and against them. It is an interactive tool for individuals and groups to use for uncovering some points of personal privilege. It helps users consider how our experiences may differ from others' and why. This exercise can range from humbling to disturbing, illuminating, and even inspiring.

5. Podcast: *Code Switch,* with Shereen Marisol Meraji, Gene Demby, Kat Chow, and others: www.npr.org /podcasts/510312/codeswitch

Based on the common tendency to switch up our language based on the race of the person(s) we are talking to, the *Code Switch* podcast takes on race- and identity-related topics that are not usually discussed in the mainstream. Their podcast team is uniquely made up of all young people of color who are enthusiastic about diving into interesting and sometimes difficult conversations about race, grounding their conversations in history and pop culture.

DIVERSIFY YOUR FEED: UNDERSTAND BLUE-STATE AMERICA

Here is a list of comedians, pundits, leaders and social analysts whom I consider voices of importance on current progressive thinking. They represent a diversity of races, nationalities, and genders, and I follow them for their unique styles and perspectives on identity and social difference.

- Wajahat Ali, @WajahatAli
- W. Kamau Bell, @wkamaubell
- Best of the Left podcast, @bestoftheleft
- Zahra Billoo, @zahrabilloo
- Senator Cory Booker (D-NJ), @CoryBooker
- Laverne Cox, @Lavernecox
- Chuck D, @MrChuckD
- RoseAnn DeMoro (executive director of National Nurses United and of the California Nurses Association/National Nurses Organizing Committee), @RoseAnnDeMoro
- Rep. Keith Ellison (D-MN), @keithellison
- Francesca Fiorentini (journalist, activist, comedian, host and producer of the show *Newsbroke* on AJ+), @franifio
- Rep. Tulsi Gabbard (D-HI), @TulsiGabbard
- Alicia Garza, @aliciagarza
- Danny Glover, @mrdannyglover
- Senator Kamala Harris (D-CA), @KamalaHarris
- Ilyse Hogue, @ilyseh
- Blair Imani, @BlairImani
- Jodi Jacobson, @jljacobson
- Clara Jeffery (editor in chief of *Mother Jones* magazine), @ClaraJeffery
- Rep. Hakeem Jeffries (D-NY), @RepJeffries
- Colin Kaepernick, @Kaepernick7

- Valarie Kaur, @valariekaur
- Shaun King, @ShaunKing
- Shelby Knox, @ShelbyKnox
- Sally Kohn, @sallykohn
- María Teresa Kumar, @MariaTeresa1
- Rep. Barbara Lee (D-CA), @RepBarbaraLee
- Annie Leonard (creator of the film *Story of Stuff,* executive director of Greenpeace), @AnnieMLeonard
- Jessica Luther, @scATX
- Pastor Michael McBride, @pastormykmac
- Janet Mock, @janetmock
- Trevor Noah (comedian and current host of *The Daily Show*), @Trevornoah
- Carmen Perez, @msladyjustice1
- Issa Rae (mixed-media content creator, writer, actress, most known for online series *Awkward Black Girl* and her HBO series, *Insecure*), @IssaRae
- Franchesca "Chescaleigh" Ramsey (YouTube personality, comedian, activist, and host of MTV's *Decoded*), @chescaleigh
- Robert Reich (longtime political commentator and educator), @RBReich
- Riese, @autowin
- Rashad Robinson, @rashadrobinson
- Senator Bernie Sanders (I-VT), @SenSanders
- Linda Sarsour, @lsarsour
- Bakari Sellers (attorney and politician from South Carolina), @Bakari_Sellers
- Yara Shahidi, @yarashahidi
- Michael Skolnik (activist, author, speaker, and entrepreneur), @MichaelSkolnik
- Jay Smooth (cultural commentator and hip-hop philosopher, most known for web series *Ill Doctrine* and hip-hop radio program *WBAI's Underground Railroad*), @jsmooth995

- Jill Soloway, @jillsoloway
- Jose Antonio Vargas, @joseiswriting
- Dawud Walid, @DawudWalid
- Senator Elizabeth Warren (D-MA), @SenWarren
- Rep. Maxine Waters (D-CA), @MaxineWaters
- Tim Wise, @timjacobwise

BE INFORMED, GET INVOLVED

Throughout this book, I have talked about organizations and efforts that are working to solve America's toughest problems. Should you want to get involved—whether through online action, volunteer work, or donations—here is a little more information about their respective missions and initiatives.

The overwhelming majority of sources on this list are liberal and progressive. But I do list some key conservative groups, as well. In no way is this a comprehensive list of all the amazing work out there—but I attempted to include something for everyone.

Political Organizations

ACLU: www.aclu.org | @ACLU

The American Civil Liberties Union is an iconic organization, fighting for civil liberties for more than one hundred years. The ACLU is not just for legal experts—it has local chapters and online actions that members can take every day.

American Conservative Union:
www.conservative.org | @ACUConservative

The ACU has been a leading voice for conservatives for more than fifty years. It develops and provides conservative positions for all levels of government and hosts one of the largest and most influential annual gathering of conservatives: CPAC. Some may be surprised to hear that their foundation has also been a very close partner of ours on criminal-justice reform.

American Enterprise Institute: www.aei.org | @AEI

The American Enterprise Institute is best known as the premier think tank among conservatives. It describes its research as "making the intellectual, moral, and practical case" for conservative values. To find the latest conservative research on any policy, this is where you turn.

Black Lives Matter:
www.blacklivesmatter.com | @Blklivesmatter

Black Lives Matter is a must-watch organization for anyone wanting to understand twenty-first-century movement-building in the age of social media. This group forever changed both how we think about social change and how we talk about race relations in the United States and worldwide.

Brennan Center for Justice:
www.brennancenter.org/ | @BrennanCenter

The Brennan Center for Justice's innovative policies have been bedrocks for liberal organizers and politicians nationwide. It covers a range of issues that blue-state America cares deeply about: voting rights, criminal-justice reform, money in politics, and more.

CAIR: www.cair.com | @CAIRNational

The Council on American-Islamic Relations defends the civil liberties of American Muslims and raises positive awareness about Islam throughout the United States. CAIR has been a powerful counterforce to Trump's proposed Muslim travel ban and Islamophobia. You can sign up for action alerts and also learn more through their conferences, seminars, and workshops.

Center for American Progress:
www.americanprogress.org | @amprog
The Center for American Progress champions progressive policies and values on every current issue in politics. They also hold frequent events on a variety of topics for folks who want to engage in thoughtful conversation on the issues of the day.

Center for Community Change:
www.communitychange.org | @communitychange
CCC is a movement-building organization—bringing people together from diverse communities to bring about social change. This coalition provides training and resources around the country. I recommend it for anyone who wants to get involved and make change.

Color of Change:
www.colorofchange.org | @ColorOfChange
Color of Change is the nation's largest online racial-justice organization by and for black people. It mobilizes its online members to respond quickly to injustice—and it wins. Color of Change was founded in 2005 when James Rucker and I emailed one thousand of our friends in the wake of Hurricane Katrina. Under the leadership of Rashad Robinson, it has become a political powerhouse.

Democracy in Color:
www.democracyincolor.com/ | @DemocracyColor
Democracy in Color is helping to empower the "New American Majority"—the multiracial, multicultural, and progressive voters

who make up a core part of the blue-state voting bloc. Its articles and podcasts are a must for understanding what matters to progressives of this demographic.

Demos: www.demos.org | @Demos_Org

Working to expand economic fairness and democracy, Demos is especially relevant at this time. I served on the board for a number of years and find the depth of its work unique. Led by Heather McGhee, Demos fights for an America that works for all of us.

Disability Rights Education and Defense Fund: www.dredf.org | @DREDF

DREDF's mission is to advance the civil and human rights of people with disabilities through legal advocacy, training, education, and public-policy and legislative development. It has resources on a range of issues and has been at the forefront of disability-rights action since 1979.

Domestic Workers United: www.domesticworkersunited.org | @DWU_NYC

Domestic Workers United organizes nannies, housekeepers, and elder caregivers to fight for fair labor standards and expand the movement to end labor exploitation for all. Its Domestic Workers' Bill of Rights is groundbreaking legislation.

The Dream Corps: www.TheDreamCorps.org | @thedreamcorps

The Dream Corps brings people together to solve America's toughest problems. Its mission is to close prison doors and open doors of opportunity. I founded this accelerator for social justice in 2015, with the aim of fighting hate with "Love + Power." The Dream Corps supports a series of initiatives, including #YesWeCode, #GreenForAll, #cut50, and #LoveArmy.

Exhale: www.exhaleprovoice.org | @ExhaleProVoice
Exhale provides a wide range of support services to women and men after abortion. They take no political stance on abortion—instead they are "pro-voice," bringing together people with different beliefs on abortion. Their model of navigating a charged issue should give hope to anyone wanting to bridge partisan divides.

Family Equality Council:
www.familyequality.org | @family_equality
"Family values" is often tagged as a conservative issue. The Family Equality Council expands that concept. It aims to represent the three million parents who are lesbian, gay, bisexual, transgender, and queer in this country and their six million children—advancing social justice for all families.

FreedomWorks:
www.freedomworks.org/ | @FreedomWorks
FreedomWorks is a go-to group for taking action on issues that matter to libertarians and conservatives. Although there are many issues we disagree on, FreedomWorks has been a key ally in the effort to reform the criminal-justice system—a true testament to the power of bipartisanship.

Greenlining Institute:
www.greenlining.org | @Greenlining
The Greenlining Institute is part research, part action. It works on a diverse set of progressive issues that share a common goal: removing barriers to opportunity for all. Its leadership programs are top-notch for people serious about making an impact for equity and justice.

Indivisible:
www.indivisibleguide.com | @IndivisibleTeam
To organize locally and take action, there is no better resource then the Indivisible website. It provides comprehensive how-to guides, action tool-kits, and local groups, to demystify activism and make it easy to be involved on political issues of the day.

The LGBT National Help Center:
www.glbthotline.org | @glbtNatlHelpCtr
The LGBT National Help Center has three national hotlines dedicated to meeting the needs of the gay, lesbian, bisexual, and transgender communities and their allies. It also maintains a list of fifteen thousand local resources across the country, and its website has an updated reading list for anyone wanting to learn more.

Muslim Advocates:
www.muslimadvocates.org | @MuslimAdvocates
Muslim Advocates is a national legal advocacy and educational organization dedicated to ensuring the right to religious freedom for all Americans. Its work has become critical in the Trump era— providing a thoughtful and representative voice for the concerns of Muslim Americans nationwide.

National Immigration Law Center:
www.nilc.org | @NILC_org
NILC defends and advances the rights of low-income immigrants. From litigation to policy advocacy to cutting-edge research, NILC confronts the country's greatest immigration challenges. It also offers practical training online and over the phone.

People's Action: www.peoplesaction.org | @PplsAction
People's Action boasts one of America's biggest and best set of or-

ganizers and volunteers—making a huge difference in their local communities. Its website always features a call to action, current news, and affiliate organizations with which to get involved.

Planned Parenthood:
www.plannedparenthood.org | @PPFA

Planned Parenthood is a women's healthcare provider, delivering affordable and vital reproductive services to more than 2.4 million people just last year. Planned Parenthood, its services, and the attacks against it have been around for one hundred years.

Revolutionary Love Project:
www.revolutionarylove.net | @valariekaur

After the 2016 election, I was truly inspired by the vision of the Revolutionary Love Project and became an active supporter. You can visit their website to sign their declaration of revolutionary love and be part of a coalition of faith and moral leaders, public voices, and organizations rising up to reclaim love as a public ethic and a way to fight for justice.

Southern Poverty Law Center:
www.splcenter.org | @splcenter

SPLC is legendary for its outstanding work in fighting hate and bigotry since 1971. Known mostly for its fierce litigation and inspiring education efforts, its work on monitoring and reporting hate crimes is especially critical at this moment.

Voto Latino: www.votolatino.org | @votolatino

Voto Latino is committed to being a megaphone for a demographic often overlooked by policymakers and politicians. Although known for its Get Out the Vote work, Voto Latino has expanded to take on other issues of importance in the Latino community—with many ways to get involved and take action.

Women's March:
www.womensmarch.com | @womensmarch

The Women's March organized the largest coordinated protest in U.S. history and one of the largest in world history—one day after Trump took office. Their diverse platform covers a range of critical issues facing the country. Visit their website to find ways to get involved and stay up-to-date on their latest campaigns and actions.

Compilation: Video News Services

The digital age has changed the way we consume news. For quick takes on news of the day, progressives turn to a few key places for videos sure to go viral. I would also recommend these to conservatives trying to understand the current progressive mood: NowThis, Fusion, AJ+, ATTN:, Mic.com.

Compilation: Conservative and Libertarian News Sources

There is a depth of news sources on the right to read online. These publications are thought leaders and a must-read for anyone exploring conservative politics, for whatever reasons: National Review, IJReview, The Federalist, Reason.com.

Criminal-Justice Reform and Drug Policy

This list is for people concerned about the opioid epidemic and the state of our criminal-justice system. Much of what I have learned over the years came from the people below—strong voices and partners dedicated to ending the era of mass incarceration.

Voices on the Left
- Lenore Anderson, @LenoreAnderson
- Jessica Jackson, @JessyMichele

- Glenn Martin, @glennEmartin
- John Pfaff, @JohnFPfaff
- Shaka Senghor, @ShakaSenghor
- Samuel Sinyangwe, @samswey
- Clint Smith, @ClintSmithIII

Voices on the Right
- Sheriff Tom Dart, @TomDart
- Fix Criminal Justice, @FixCrimJustice
- Dan Isett, @DanIsett
- Marc Levin, @MarcALevin
- Pat Nolan, @PatNolan4Justic
- Jason Pye, @pye

Advocates for Opioid Recovery:
www.opioidrecovery.org | @AORecovery
Advocates for Opioid Recovery is a bipartisan effort that I advise with Newt Gingrich and Patrick Kennedy. We are dedicated to advancing a science-based, evidence-based treatment system that can reduce death and suffering from opioid addiction. It is a great source for the latest news and policy dealing with this growing crisis.

Alliance for Safety and Justice:
www.allianceforsafetyandjustice.org | @SafeAndJustUSA
The Alliance for Safety and Justice (ASJ) is a national organization that aims to win new safety priorities in states across the country. ASJ partners with leaders and advocates to advance state reform; it also brings together diverse crime survivors to advance policies that help communities most harmed by crime and violence. Founded by Lenore Anderson, ASJ is the sister organization of Californians for Safety and Justice.

Clergy for a New Drug Policy:
www.newdrugpolicy.org | @ClergyNDP

Clergy for a New Drug Policy works with voices of faith across the country seeking to end the war on drugs. They are truly multi-faith and offer a variety of ways for people of faith to take action on drug policy.

#cut50: www.cut50.org | @cut_50

#cut50 is a national bipartisan initiative that I co-founded with Jessica Jackson and Matt Haney. From policy, direct service, story-telling, and organizing, there are multiple ways to be involved in criminal-justice reform—on both the federal and local levels. #cut50 is powered by the Dream Corps.

Drug Policy Alliance:
www.drugpolicy.org | @DrugPolicyOrg

Drug Policy Alliance brings together a broad coalition of groups working to reform drug policy in the United States. They have had major legislative victories and offer clear actions and "activist tool-kits" for anyone looking to get involved in the issue.

Ella Baker Center for Human Rights:
www.ellabakercenter.org | @ellabakercenter

The Ella Baker Center is a group I co-founded in 1996 to coordinate lawsuits against unlawful police violence. More than twenty years later, it is still going strong—leading fights on criminal-justice reform, policing, and local community issues in Oakland, California. The Ella Baker Center has helped to close five abusive youth prisons and successfully blocked the construction of a super-jail for youth in Oakland, California.

Equal Justice Initiative: www.eji.org | @eji_org

Since 1989, Bryan Stevenson and Equal Justice Initiative have been on the forefront of putting a story and face to the heartbreaking realities of the criminal-justice system in the United States. Its resources are must-reads for anyone wanting to learn more and be deeply connected to the issue.

Facing Addiction in America:
www.facingaddiction.org | @FacingAddiction

Facing Addiction has resources, events, and actions for anyone who has been impacted by addiction. They have a variety of ways to join and make a difference on this issue.

Families Against Mandatory Minimums:
www.famm.org | @FAMMFoundation

FAMM is a nonpartisan organization fighting to reform mandatory-minimum sentencing nationwide. Its work is compelling and effective—changing both federal and state laws. FAMM highlights the human costs of excessive incarceration with stories and videos from impacted individuals and families.

Harm Reduction Coalition:
www.harmreduction.org | @HarmReduction

Harm Reduction Coalition works across the country to ensure that drug-treatment policies prioritize healthcare and health crises over punishment and stigma. It provides direct service and training to people and organizations interested in reducing the harm from drug abuse and addiction.

Just Leadership USA:
www.justleadershipusa.org | @JustLeadersUSA

Just Leadership USA is a national network of formerly incarcerated and personally impacted individuals fighting back against mass incarceration. Regardless of where you live, you can get involved in its advocacy campaigns or apply for one of its leadership training programs.

Justice Roundtable:
www.justiceroundtable.org | @justiceroundtab
Led by Nkechi Taifa and the Open Society Foundation, the Justice Roundtable is a coalition of groups, primarily based in Washington, D.C., that works on federal criminal-justice policy. You can attend one of their quarterly meetings or join a working group to advance the mission for true reform.

National Association for Drug Court Professionals:
www.allrise.org | @_ALLRISE_
NADCP is a national resource and advocacy group for drug-court professionals—judges, prosecutors, defense attorneys, and clinical workers—from the more than three thousand drug courts in the United States. Its campaigns champion commonsense reforms to empower drug-using people to change their lives.

Pretrial Justice Institute: www.pretrial.org | @Pretrial
The Pretrial Justice Institute advocates nationwide for smart and safe reforms in pretrial practices. There is a dangerous human cost to keeping unconvicted people behind bars—PJI has a variety of initiatives worthy of your support.

Right on Crime:
www.rightoncrime.com | @RightOnCrime
Right on Crime captures the depth and breadth of what criminal-justice reform means to the conservative movement. If you had to credit one organization for the growing commitment on the right to fix our prison system, that organization would be Right on Crime. Its guiding principles are a must-read for anyone working

for reform in a bipartisan manner. And most important, it has been behind some of the most comprehensive criminal-justice reforms in red states to date.

Vera Institute of Justice: www.vera.org | @verainstitute

The Vera Institute houses one of the most comprehensive set of resources on all aspects of the criminal-justice system. Most of its work is available online. Its research informs their projects and policy—very creative, compelling, and effective.

Twenty-first-Century Jobs: Clean Tech

Healing the land and the cities will take a concerted effort from every sector of society. The people below all work from different angles to ensure a just transition from a pollution-based economy to one powered mainly by cleaner energy sources. Environmental protection and job creation should go hand in hand—and these individuals and organizations are making it possible.

- Mustafa Ali, @EJinAction
- Gilbert Campbell, @gilbertcampbell
- Gil Friend, @gfriend
- Al Gore, @algore
- Annie Leonard, @AnnieMLeonard
- Bill McKibben, @billmckibben
- Michelle Romero, @michelledreams2
- Jonah Sachs, @jonahsachs
- Ariel Schwartz, @arielhs
- Tom Steyer, @tomsteyer
- Vien Truong, @viendetta
- Commissioner Karmenu Vella, @KarmenuVella
- Rev. Lennox Yearwood, @RevYearwood

Asian Pacific Environmental Network:
www.apen4ej.org | @APEN4EJ

APEN is a model for organizations that want to do deep local work in their communities. APEN has been leading the way in community engagement for policy change—and proving that good environmental solutions are also good for the economy.

Appalachian Regional Commission:
www.arc.gov | @ARCgov

The Appalachian Regional Commission is a coalition of federal, state, and local governments dedicated to growing the economy and infrastructure of the region while protecting the environment and the health of their citizens.

Climate Justice Alliance:
www.ourpowercampaign.org | @CJAOurPower

Climate Justice Alliance is a national coalition committed to just transition work. Its "Our Power" campaign is proving that meaningful employment and environmental progress can and should go hand in hand. In pilot communities around the country, Our Power has already seen great success.

Evangelical Environmental Network:
www.creationcare.org | @CreationCare

Rooted in their Christian faith, the Evangelical Environmental Network is made up of individuals and churches united in caring for the environment. They have a number of different calls to action and prayers to offer their members.

Green For All: www.greenforall.org | @GreenForAll

I founded Green For All in 2007 and still work with them today. In the beginning, just the idea that we could build an inclusive green economy that lifted people out of poverty was new. Today,

Green For All has a long list of victories and continues to build on its success with innovative campaigns and programs.

Greenpeace: www.greenpeace.org | @Greenpeace
Greenpeace is an iconic organization for environmental action. Although founded in the 1970s, Greenpeace is incredibly relevant, with cutting-edge creativity and messaging. They have a robust intern and volunteer program for folks wanting to be more involved.

Indigenous Environmental Network: www.ienearth.org | @IENearth
Using traditional knowledge and natural laws, the Indigenous Environmental Network organizes campaigns and builds public awareness to protect the environment. Their network provides services for and is made up of individual indigenous leaders, community organizations, and tribal governments.

Interfaith Power & Light: www.interfaithpowerandlight.org | @interfaithpower
Interfaith Power & Light is a religious response to global warming. They work on the individual, community, and state- and federal-policy efforts. Big and growing—a local IPL congregation may be near you. If not, they have actions online for any person of faith working on environmental issues.

Kentuckians for the Commonwealth: www.kftc.org | @kftc
Kentuckians for the Commonwealth is a statewide initiative aimed at building "New Power" for Kentuckians. This group brings campaigns for an inclusive green economy to a red state—and they are winning. Statewide chapters and leadership programs make it easy to get involved with KFTC.

NextGen America:
www.nextgenamerica.org | @NextGenAmerica

NextGen Climate is a political organization combating climate change. It has resources for people who want to learn more and actions for people who want to influence policy.

Sierra Club: www.sierraclub.org | @SierraClub

Founded in 1892 and with more than three million members, the Sierra Club is one of the biggest and oldest organizations working on environmental issues. With chapters all around the country, it is easy to get involved in your local community.

Union of Concerned Scientists:
www.ucsusa.org | @UCSUSA

Union of Concerned Scientists takes a rigorous scientific approach to solving the world's toughest problems. Its programs are known for both their innovation and practicality. UCS also maintains a list of compelling actions based on cutting-edge research (and tips and tools to be effective in your actions).

U.S. Climate Action Network:
www.usclimatenetwork.org | @uscan

The U.S. Climate Action Network is an alliance of more than one hundred seventy organizations working together to fight against climate change. Its list of member organizations is a great resource for anyone wanting to get involved.

Twenty-first-Century Jobs: High Tech

Our movement toward high-tech employment has already begun. These folks are at the forefront of creating a future that includes everyone.

- Kwame Anku, @kwameyaoanku
- Byron Auguste, @byron_auguste
- Tricia Bobeda, @triciabobeda
- Kimberly Bryant, @6Gems
- Angie Coleman, @angieidunno
- Tanya DePass, @cypheroftyr
- Felix Flores, Jr., @felixnotalex
- Soha Kareem, @sokareemie
- Emily Reichert, @EmilyLReichert
- Reshma Saujani, @reshmasaujani
- Ramesh Srinivasan, @rameshmedia
- Shawn Wilson, @shhwilson

Bit Source: www.bitsourceky.com | @bitsourceky
If you ever need any web or software-development help, Bit Source is a great place to support. They are putting coal country back to work in high-tech jobs. Through their efforts, a revitalization is starting—one I urge we must continue for a "just transition."

Black Girls Code:
www.blackgirlscode.com | @BlackGirlsCode
Black Girls Code was one of the first on the scene with training programs for young kids overlooked in the STEM fields. You can both sign your kid up and volunteer to help at their trainings and programs nationwide.

Bootcamps
Coding "bootcamps" are training programs to get you job-ready in the tech sector in a short amount of time—without requiring a college diploma. They exist all over the country and serve different demographics. If you want to start pursuing a career in the tech sector, here are three bootcamps to start exploring:

- Galvanize | www.galvanize.com | @galvanize
- General Assembly | generalassembly | @GA
- Hack Reactor | www.hackreactor.com | @hackreactor

Code.org: www.code.org | @codeorg

Code.org partners with school districts around the country to bring computer-science curriculum into K–12 classrooms. If your child is getting a computer-science education, code.org may be why. Its online platform has free resources for everyone, and there are many ways to get involved in bringing their work to your district.

Code 2040: www.code2040.org | @Code2040

Code 2040 is a vital pipeline organization—getting talented minority STEM students into the biggest tech firms. Prospective participants, donors, and career mentors are always needed.

Girls Who Code: girlswhocode.com | @GirlsWhoCode

Free summer programs and after-school clubs around the country make Girls Who Code one of the biggest and most successful organizations fighting the gender gap in technology. There is sure to be a program near you—or, if not, you can bring one to your local community.

Level Playing Field Institute: www.lpfi.org | @LPFI

Level Playing Field is part of the legendary Kapor Center for Social Impact—one of the first places to address racial disparity in the tech sector. It is also a go-to place for research in the field. Their summer program (SMASH) is amazing for future leaders of the field.

Mined Minds: www.minedminds.org | @MinedMinds

Mined Mines is building tech hubs in red states—currently in West Virginia and southwest Pennsylvania. It offers free coding courses in coordination with local community colleges. It has invested heavily in building local talent while breaking barriers in the tech field.

Tech Inclusion: techinclusion.co | @techinclusionco

Tech Inclusion seeks to improve diversity and inclusion in the tech sector. It hosts conferences, start-up showcases, career fairs, and forums across the nation and across the world—offering many opportunities to connect in the field.

#YesWeCode: www.yeswecode.org | @YesWeCode

#YesWeCode is the organization I co-founded with Prince. It will always be near and dear to my heart. Our goal is to get one hundred thousand underrepresented folks careers in the tech sectors. We award scholarships and both run and advise bootcamps, with an emphasis on the inclusion of people of color, women, and individuals of modest means.

ACKNOWLEDGMENTS

FIRST OF ALL, MY PARENTS: LORETTA JEAN KIRKENDOLL Jones and the late Willie Anthony Jones. Also, my late maternal grandparents: C.M.E. Bishop Chester Arthur Kirkendoll and Alice Elizabeth Singleton Kirkendoll. Those four people gave me the best foundation that any black kid who grew up on the edge of a small Tennessee town could hope for.

My wife, Jana Carter, and our sons, Cabral and Mattai, have made untold sacrifices for me to create this book—and to do the work that underlies it. No words can ever express my love or convey my appreciation for all of them.

I salute my entire family: the Kirkendolls, the Carters, and the legendary Smith-Jones-Glover clan of Memphis; my twin sister, Angela Thracheryl Jones, and her sons, DeAubrey Jerome Weekly and Brandon Demetrious Weekly; my godparents—Dorothy Zellner, Constancia "Dinky" Romilly, and Terry Weber; my godsister, Diana Frappier; and my goddaughter, Damaris Lewis. Rest in peace to my uncle, Leland Kapel Kirkendoll, who died this year.

I am especially grateful for the friendship of Monica Elizabeth Peek, Karen Streeter, Kimaria Seymour, Michelle Loren Alexander, Rinku Sen, Ai-jen Poo, Lea Endres, Nina Utne, Noland Chambliss, Phaedra Ellis-Lamkins, Craig Harshaw, Arnold Perkins, Deborah James, Harmony Goldberg, Gihan Perera, James Rucker, Marianne Manilov, Omarr Baker, Tyka Nelson, Steve Silton, Michael Lythcott, Valerie Aubel, the entire Vin Ryan family, Lama Tsomo, Rashad Robinson, Colin Holtz, Reggie Hudlin, Dexter King, Nancy Lublin, Joi Ito, Abby Disney, Alicia Garza, Sharon Alpert, Viktoria Modesta, Ava DuVernay, Jill Kershaw, Leigh Blake, Aimee Christenson, Byron Auguste, U.S. Rep. Tulsi Gabbard, Kerry Kennedy, Lauryn Hill, Alicia Keys, Michael Bearden, Arianna Huffington, and Reid Hoffman. I will always salute Eva Jefferson Paterson for helping me launch my legal career when nobody else would give me a job.

I am honored to be a co-founder of many institutions. I thank everyone who has helped to build the Ella Baker Center for Human Rights, Color of Change, Green For All, and Rebuild the Dream (which is now TheDreamCorps.org). I am indebted to the staff, donors, and board of the Dream Corps, which today supports #YesWeCode, #cut50, Green For All, and the #LoveArmy. Special thanks to early partners who supported my ideas: Maxine Williams, Andrea Hoffman, Richard Branson, Jean Olewang, Amy Henderson, Cheryl Contee, Gina Bianchini, Norm Pearlstine, Mattie McFadden-Lawson and Michael Lawson, Jamie Wong, Elijah Allan-Blitz, Tom Steyer, Mark Holden, and the Rev. Jesse Jackson.

I am forever in debt to CNN—especially Jeff Zucker, Amy Entelis, Rebecca Kutler, and the amazing team of journalists and commentators on both sides of the aisle there.

Ditto for the whole team at Magic Labs Media and Messy Truth.com. Documentary filmmakers Brandon and Lance Kramer at Meridian Hill Pictures have been our first-rate partners.

I am proud to be managed by Roc Nation and represented by

both William Morris Endeavor and the Creative Artists Agency. Hats off to my book agent, Gail Ross.

This book would have been impossible to create without the hard work and support of Sarah Fuchs, Jamel Brinkley, Jean Ho, Aaron Schulman, and Natalie Eilbert. I appreciate Marnie Cochran at Random House for her patience and persistence.

I want to give special acknowledgment to three conservative white guys—my high school buddy Ken Hartley, my college professor E. Jerald Ogg, and my partner in criminal-justice and opioid-policy reform, Newt Gingrich. All three have shown me innumerable kindnesses and taught me invaluable lessons. All three relationships are proof that shared ideology is no prerequisite for a shared sense of mission, a shared faith in our Creator, or a shared love of country.

I am happy to note that this book, *Beyond The Messy Truth,* is the first literary co-production of Magic Labs Media, LLC.

In closing, I again dedicate this book to Priya Haji and Prince Rogers Nelson—two dear friends, both gone too soon.

ABOUT THE AUTHOR

VAN JONES rose to fame as a CNN political contributor and host of the recurring CNN prime-time special *The Messy Truth with Van Jones*. A graduate of the University of Tennessee at Martin and Yale Law School, he was a special adviser to the Obama White House and is the author of two *New York Times* bestsellers. Jones founded the social-justice accelerator the Dream Corps. He has built and led numerous social-justice and pro-ecology enterprises, including the Ella Baker Center for Human Rights, Color of Change, and Green For All. He has earned many honors, including the World Economic Forum's "Young Global Leader" designation, *Rolling Stone*'s "12 Leaders Who Get Things Done," *Fast Company*'s "12 Most Creative Minds On Earth," a Webby Special Achievement Award, and *Time*'s "100 Most Influential People in the World." He is the founder and CEO of Magic Labs Media, LLC, which runs MessyTruth.com. Van lives with his wife and two children in the Los Angeles area.

vanjones.net
Facebook.com/vanjones
Twitter: @VanJones68
Instagram: @vanjones68

ABOUT THE TYPE

This book was set in Fairfield, the first typeface from the hand of the distinguished American artist and engraver Rudolph Ruzicka (1883–1978). Ruzicka was born in Bohemia (in the present-day Czech Republic) and came to America in 1894. He set up his own shop, devoted to wood engraving and printing, in New York in 1913 after a varied career working as a wood engraver, in photoengraving and banknote printing plants, and as an art director and freelance artist. He designed and illustrated many books, and was the creator of a considerable list of individual prints—wood engravings, line engravings on copper, and aquatints.